The Big Book of
Music
Games

By Debra Olson Pressnall
& Lorilee Malecha

Cover Illustration by
Margo De Paulis

Inside Illustrations by
Becky Radtke, Julie Anderson,
Rex Schneider & Valery Larson

Publisher
Instructional Fair • TS Denison
Grand Rapids, Michigan 49544

Permission to Reproduce

Dedication

To our husbands, Tim Malecha and Steven Pressnall,
for all their love and support

Credits

Authors: Debra Olson Pressnall
    & Lorilee Malecha
Cover Artist: Margo De Paulis
Inside Illustrations: Becky Radtke,
    Julie Anderson, Rex Schneider
    & Valery Larson
Project Director/Editor:
    Debra Olson Pressnall
Editor: Danielle de Gregory
Cover Art Production: Darcy Bell-Myers
Graphic Layout: Deborah Hanson McNiff

About the Authors

As a music specialist, choir director, and piano teacher, Lorilee J. Malecha has taught for more than eight years at Randolph Public Schools, Randolph, Minnesota and loved music for much, much longer. In her free time, she enjoys creating new materials to reinforce music fundamentals. She has a B.A. in music education from Southwest State University, Marshall, Minnesota.

Debra Olson Pressnall has 12 years of experience as an elementary teacher and over 10 years of experience in the field of educational publishing. Her interest in music started as a young girl with piano, and continued with flute, and vocal lessons. A graduate of Concordia College, Moorhead, Minnesota, she has a B.S. in elementary education with a music minor.

Standard Book Number: 1-56822-673-X
The Big Book of Music Games
Copyright © 1998 by Instructional Fair • TS Denison
2400 Turner Avenue NW
Grand Rapids, Michigan 49544

Table of Contents

Introduction

Brimming with active learning games and reproducible board games, *The Big Book of Music Games* offers a wealth of materials that strengthen basic music concepts and reading skills. Through these games students have opportunities to practice identifying notes, rests, and other commonly studied symbols as well as notes on treble and bass staves. In addition, students learn facts about famous composers with trivia games and practice identifying familiar instruments through bingo-type games.

This book is written for busy music specialists and classroom teachers who would like to provide unique materials that help their students master music fundamentals. With these reproducible pattern pages you can easily create board games on file folders, music dice from paper milk cartons, bingo cards, and much more. All of the games are made from readily-available materials. Before starting the preparation for a game, check the material list to find out which common items are needed. A few games need game markers that can be made from milk jug or water jug caps. Perhaps the board game you selected only needs a pencil and paper clip for a spinner. To make the selected game just reproduce the pattern pages on white or colored copier paper or construction paper. If desired, use watercolor markers to decorate the game cards and/or game board. When finished, mount the game cards on construction paper and/or game board on a file folder. You may prefer to laminate all game materials for durability.

As you peruse the pattern pages and read the game instructions, perhaps new game ideas come to mind. You can easily modify any of the pattern pages to meet the needs of your students or use the adorable artwork to create your own games.

We hope you have fun creating your new game materials. How you structure the games will depend on the needs and interests of your students. You may be interested in producing several sets of the same game or maybe just one copy for use in a learning center. Just select the appropriate game for reinforcing skills when you only have a few minutes of instruction time remaining during a class period or use several games for the entire class time when your students are ready for a change of pace.

Music Alphabet

Music Alphabet

Memory Match

Players: 2 or more
Object: To collect the most pairs of cards
Materials: Pattern pages 8-9, scissors, construction paper, glue, markers

Preparation: Reproduce two copies of the pattern pages and color them as desired. Mount the copies on construction paper and then cut apart the cards.

Directions: For this memory game, the children must be able to identify the letter and instrument on each card before collecting the identical cards. To begin play, arrange the cards *face down* on a large flat surface in several rows. Have the first player turn two cards *face up.* If the cards match, the player keeps the cards and then turns two more cards *face up.* If the cards do not match, the player turns the cards *face down* again. Be sure all players see the cards before they are returned to their original positions. The next player takes a turn to find matching pairs. The game ends when all possible matches have been made. If a Wild Card is turned over, the player collects both cards shown at that time.

Variation: Are you seeking ways to challenge some children? Invite those children to play "Keyboard Memory Match." Provide two copies of the game card patterns on pages 16 and 17 as well as the Wild Card on page 8 for the children to use.

Alphabet Presto!

Players: Teams of 7 children
Object: To arrange the cards in the correct musical sequence
Materials: Pattern pages 8-9, scissors, construction paper, glue, large open area

Preparation: Here is a game that can be played by small groups of children or the entire class. To prepare the materials, make one set of cards for each team of players. Photocopy the pattern pages and then mount them on construction paper. Cut out the cards. For calling cards, cut out seven 2" square pieces of construction paper and print the letters A–G on the squares.

Directions: Divide the entire class into teams of seven children. Locate an area where the children can sit and also stand as a group. Give each team a set of cards and have the members distribute the cards among themselves. Now you are ready to play "Alphabet Presto!" To begin the first round, the "Caller" draws one of the calling cards and announces the letter. For example, the card is "F." The player who holds "F" for each team moves to a large open area. On the signal "Go," the other team players who hold cards must arrange themselves in order after the letter "F" to complete the musical sequence of letters. For example, F, G, A, B, C, D, and E. When finished, give each team a point for completing the arrangement correctly. Have the children return to their teams' locations and place their cards in the draw pile. At this time, a member of each team shuffles the cards and distributes them again. Continue each round in the same manner.

What's That Note?

Players: 2 or 3
Object: The first player to reach "Stop" is the winner.
Materials: Pattern pages 10–13, scissors, construction paper, colored file folder, game markers, glue, watercolor markers, game marker for each player

Preparation: To make the game board, photocopy pattern pages 12-13 and color them as desired. Mount the copies to a file folder (opened flat). Photocopy the game cards on construction paper. Laminate all pieces for durability. Cut apart the cards and store them in a large envelope.

♪A ♪B ♪C ♪D ♪E ♪F ♪G♪

Directions: To start this game, give each player a game marker. Shuffle the cards and place them *face down* in a draw pile. The first player takes a card and announces the answer. If the other players think the answer is correct, the player places a marker on the corresponding note. The second player takes a turn and draws a card. When the answer is given, the player moves his or her game marker to the nearest corresponding space. If that answer is already covered with a game marker, the player loses that turn. Continue the game by playing each round in the same manner. Play ends when someone lands on the last "G" near AWESOME.

Variation: Provide copies of the keyboard note pattern cards on pages 16-17 as game cards for the students to use. Play the game in the same manner by having the players identify the "starred" note on each card and then move their game markers to the first corresponding spaces.

Wacky Keyboard

Players: 2
Object: To place game markers on 3 keys in a row
Materials: Pattern pages 14-15, file folder, glue, pencil, paper clip, game markers

Preparation: Make a copy of the pattern pages and then color them as desired. Mount the copies on the file folder.

Directions: For this game, students must not only identify the keys but devise their own strategies to win. To begin play, let the first player hold the pencil on the center of the dial and spin the paper clip. (See the illustration.)  The player reads the letter indicated by the paper clip and places a game marker on the corresponding key. The other player continues in the same manner. If the key is marked, the player loses that turn. As players place game markers on the keys, they must think about which keys to cover when choices can be made. The game ends when one player covers three keys in a row.

ABC Lineup

Players: 2
Object: The first player to fill the spaces in a grid is the winner.
Materials: Pattern pages 18-19, colored file folder, glue, 21 game pieces (milk jug caps, water jug caps, or tagboard squares), watercolor markers, black permanent marker

Preparation: For the game board, duplicate a copy of the pattern pages and then color them as desired. Mount each copy on one panel of the file folder. To prepare the game pieces, print the letters A–G on the top of the plastic caps with a permanent marker. Make three sets of the music alphabet for the players to use with the game board.

Directions: Let the players take turns drawing game pieces and placing them in the corresponding spaces on the grids. When a player has covered an entire grid, the game ends. Clear the boards and have the players start another game.

Seven-Up!

Players: 2
Object: To arrange 8 letters in the musical sequence
Materials: Pattern page 20, construction paper, 24 game pieces (milk jug caps, water jug caps, or tagboard circles), glue

Preparation: Make two copies of the pattern, then mount them on construction paper. Print each letter of the music alphabet three times on the game pieces.

Directions: Have the players set their game boards and game pieces (*face down*) on a flat surface. Each player draws a game piece and places it on the "starred" circle. (Each player has a different letter to start.) This establishes the sequence of the letters. Now the players take turns by drawing letters and placing them in the corresponding spaces until one player has completed his or her game board.

note before C	note before A	Do not move!
note before D	2 notes before C	2 notes before B
note before E	2 notes before D	Take a rest!
note before F	2 notes before E	Move to E.
note before G	2 notes before F	Move to D.

note after C	note after B	note after A
note after D	2 notes after C	2 notes before B
note after E	2 notes after D	Jump ahead 7 notes.
note after F	2 notes after E	Go back to D.
note after G	2 notes after F	Go back to A.

What's That Note?

Awesome!

Wacky Keyboard Game

F

D

Take a Rest!

A

F   D

C   G

E   B

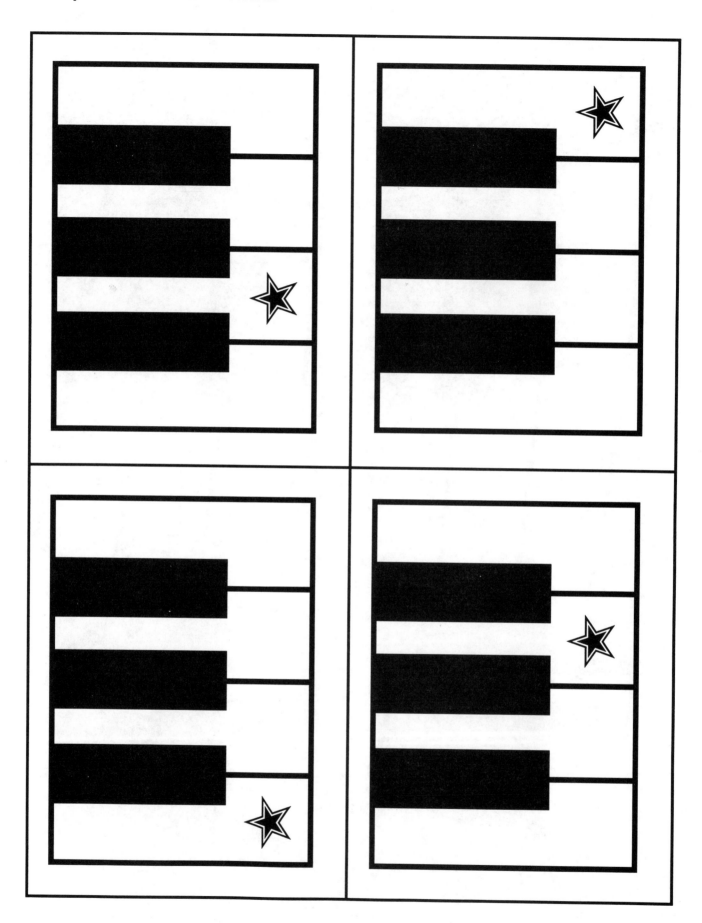

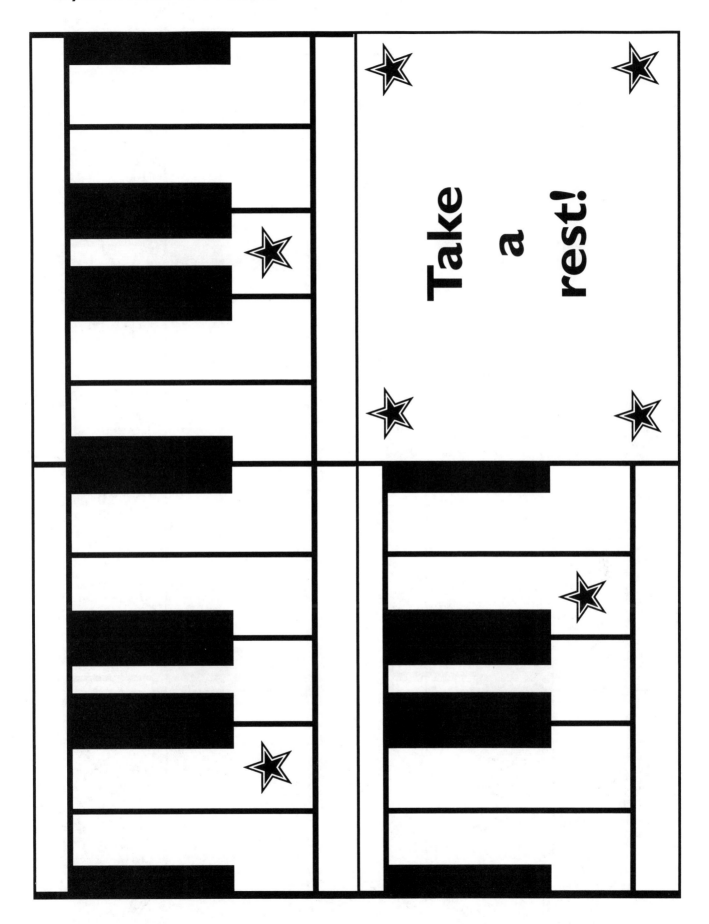

♪ A B C Lineup ♪

	A	
		G
A		

		F
	C	
C		

D		
		A
	C	

		C
E		
	A	

Music Syllables

Music Syllables

Music Syllables Memory Match

Players: 2 or more
Object: To collect the most pairs of cards
Materials: Pattern pages 24-25 or 26-27, scissors, construction paper, glue, watercolor markers

Preparation: Reproduce two copies of the pattern pages and color them as desired. Mount the copies on construction paper and then cut apart the cards.

Directions: This memory match game can be played in three different ways. Some children may need lots of practice in discriminating the different hand signs. Give these children the hand sign cards for this game. Other children can easily handle matching the hand sign with the corresponding "animal" syllable card. Provide a copy of each set of cards for these children. Finally, some children might prefer to match "animal" syllable cards during the game. To begin play, arrange the cards *face down* on a large flat surface in several rows. Have the first player turn two cards *face up*. If the cards match, the player keeps the pair of cards and then turns two more cards *face up*. If the cards do not match, the player turns the cards *face down* again. Be sure all players view the cards before they are returned to their original positions. The next player takes a turn to find matching pairs. The game ends when all possible matches have been made. If a Wild Card is turned over, the player collects both cards shown at that time.

Variation: For a more difficult game, remove the names of the syllables on the hand sign cards. Let the children collect matching pairs by matching the hand signs with the "animal" syllable cards.

Syllable Presto!

Players: Teams of 7 children
Object: To arrange the cards in the correct musical sequence

Materials: Pattern pages 24-25, scissors, tagboard, glue, large open area

Preparation: When preparing the materials for this game, determine how many teams of seven children will be formed. For each team, photocopy the pattern pages and then mount them on tagboard. Be sure to prepare an extra "Do" for each team. Cut out the cards. For "Caller" cards, cut out seven 2"-square pieces of construction paper and print the syllables (Do, Re, Mi, Fa, Sol, La, Ti) on the squares.

Directions: Divide the entire class into teams of seven children. Give each team a set of cards. To play the game, distribute the cards among team members. Now you are ready to play "Syllable Presto." Be sure to clear an area for the players to stand. Have each team sit in a circle with the game cards turned *face down* in the center. When ready to begin the first round, let each player pick a card. The Caller draws one of the special cards and announces the syllable. For example, the card is "Re." The player who holds "Re" for each team moves to a large open area. On the signal "Go," the other team players who hold cards must arrange themselves in order after the syllable "Re" to complete the musical sequence up to "Do." For example: Re, Mi, Fa, Sol, La, Ti, and Do. When finished, give each team a point for completing the arrangement correctly. Have the children return to their teams' locations and place their cards in the draw pile. Continue each round in the same manner.

Do-Re-Mi Bingo

Players: Entire class (30 students)
Object: The first player to cover 3 spaces in a row is the winner.
Materials: Pattern pages 28–43, scissors, construction paper, game markers, glue

Preparation: Photocopy the bingo card patterns. Mount the copies on construction paper, then cut apart

the cards. Duplicate two copies of pattern page 44 for the "Caller," then cut apart one copy of the cards.

Directions: If appropriate, ask one student to be the Caller. To begin play, have the Caller draw a card and announce the syllable. Each player marks the corresponding space on his or her bingo board. Continue playing in this manner until someone covers three spaces in a vertical, horizontal, or diagonal row. The students may also play until the entire board is marked.

Musical Fingers

Players: 3 or 4
Object: To identify each hand sign on the playing cards
Materials: Pattern pages 45–48, scissors, construction paper, 21 playing pieces (milk jug caps, water jug caps, or tagboard circles), permanent black marker

Preparation: Duplicate the pattern pages, then mount them on construction paper. Prepare the game pieces by printing each music syllable (Do, Re, Mi, Fa, Sol, La, Ti) three times on game pieces.

Directions: To play the game, have the players place the game pieces *face down* in the center of the playing area. Each player selects a game card. The first player draws a game piece and then matches it with the corresponding hand sign. If a match cannot be made, the game piece is returned to the draw pile. The other players take turns in the same manner until someone has made four matches on his or her game card. When starting a new game, let the players exchange game cards before beginning the first round.

Do-Re-Mi Treasure Hunt

Players: 2 or 3
Object: The first player to reach the treasure chest is the winner
Materials: Pattern pages 49–52, scissors, construction paper, file folder, game markers, glue, watercolor markers

Preparation: For the game board, photocopy pattern pages 50-51 and color them as desired. To mount the copies on a colored file folder (opened flat), trim the pages and then align them on the file folder to complete the game path. Secure in place by gluing. For the game cards, mount photocopies of card patterns on construction paper, then cut apart the cards. If desired, laminate all pieces for durability. Store the game cards along with a copy of the answer key in a large envelope.

Directions: To start this game, give each player a game marker. Shuffle the cards and place them *face down* in a draw pile. The first player takes a card and identifies the hand sign. If the other players think the answer is correct, the player places a marker on the nearest corresponding syllable. The second player takes a turn and draws a card. When the answer is given, the player moves his or her game marker to the nearest corresponding space. If that answer is already covered with a game marker, the player loses that turn. Continue the game by playing each round in the same manner. Play ends when someone reaches the treasure chest.

Variation: Use game cards on page 53.

Seven-Up!

Players: 2
Object: To arrange the music syllables correctly
Materials: Pattern page 54, 14 game pieces for each game board (milk jug caps, water jug caps or tagboard circles), construction paper, glue

Preparation: Make one copy of the game board pattern for each player. Mount the copy on construction paper. Print each music syllable twice on the game pieces.

Directions: Have the players set their game boards and game pieces (*face down*) on a flat surface. The first player draws a game piece and places it on the corresponding space after "Do." The other player continues in the same manner. *Note:* Remember the spaces will be filled in random order. Continue playing in the same manner. The first player to cover all seven spaces after "Do" says "Seven-up!" to end the game.

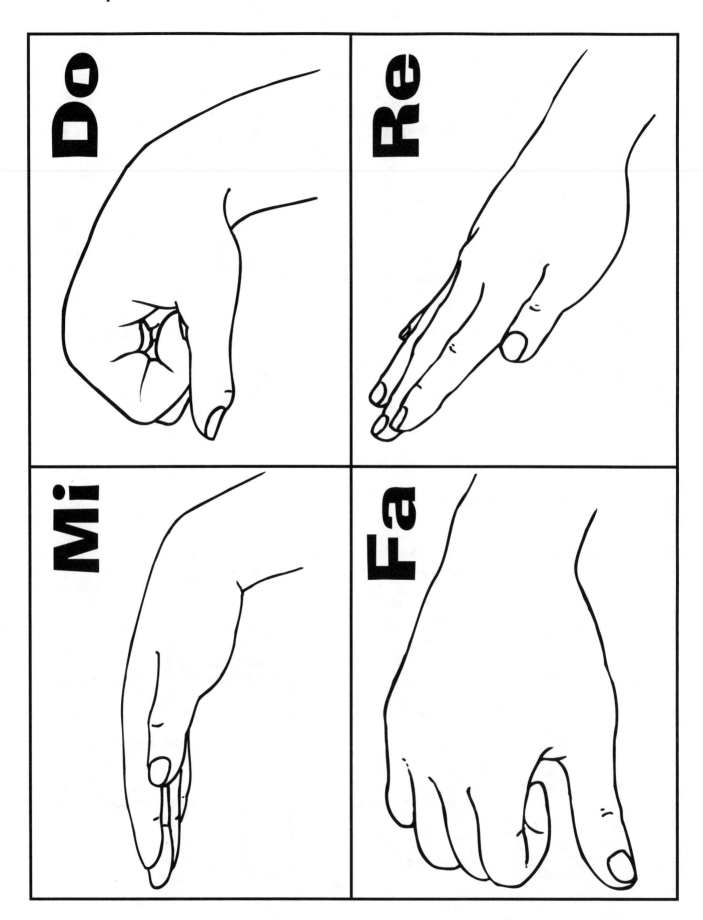

Music Syllables Card Patterns

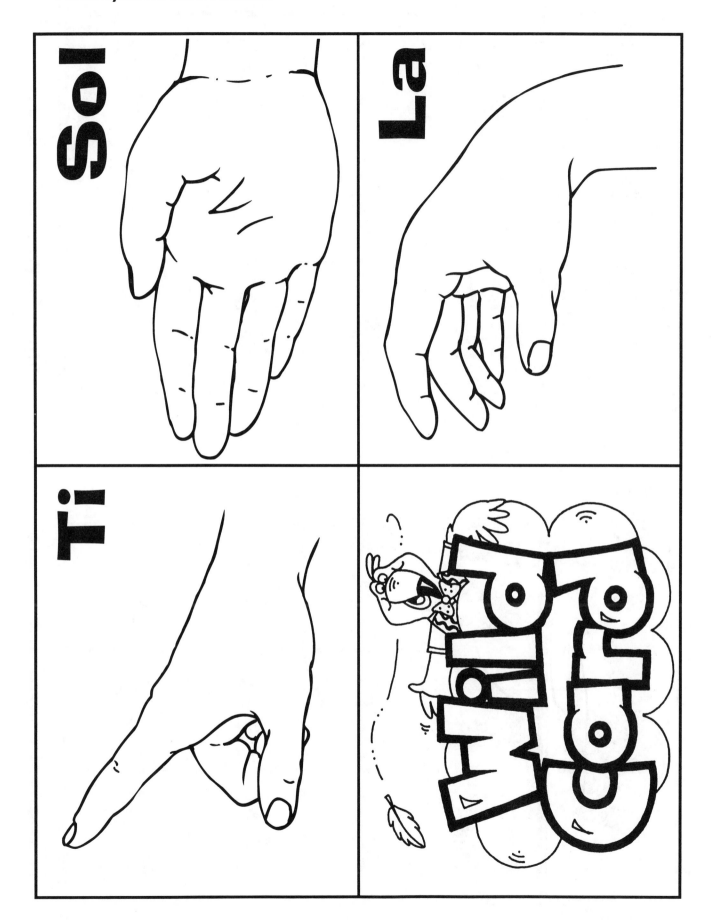

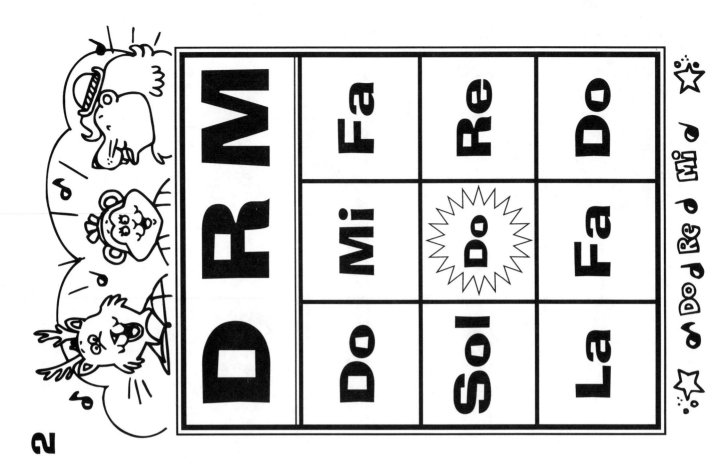

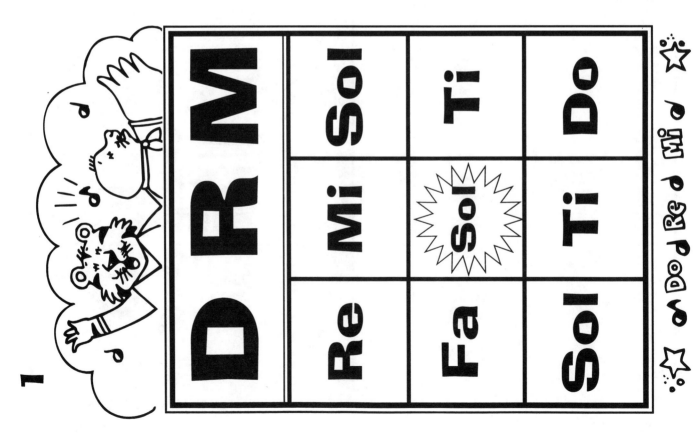

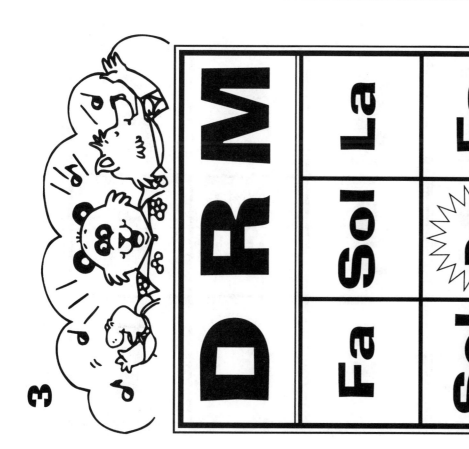

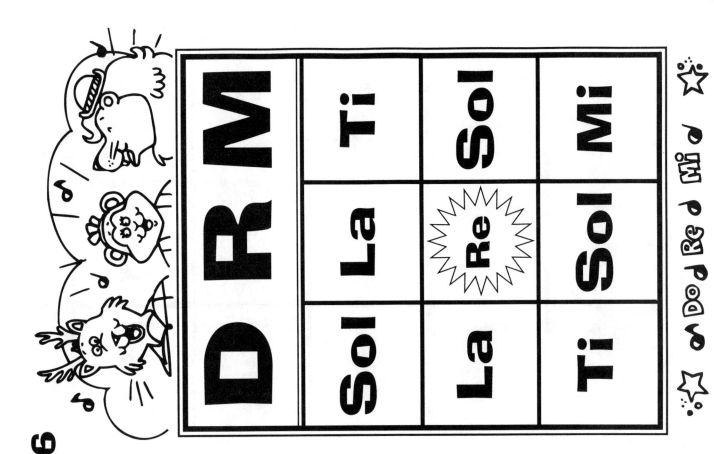

6

D R M		
Ti	Sol	Mi
Sol La	Re	Ti Sol
Sol	La	Ti

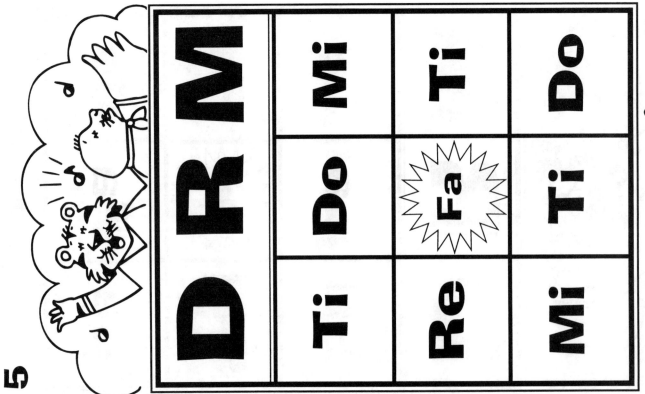

5

D R M		
Mi	Ti	Do
Ti Do	Fa	Ti Do
Ti	Re	Mi

8

D R M		
Fa Sol	Fa	Mi
Mi	Ti	Fa
Do	Sol Mi	Sol

Do Re Mi

7

D R M		
Ti	La	Sol
Fa	Sol	Ti
Do	Fa	Re

Do Re Mi

IF20453 *Big Book of Music Games*

10

D R M

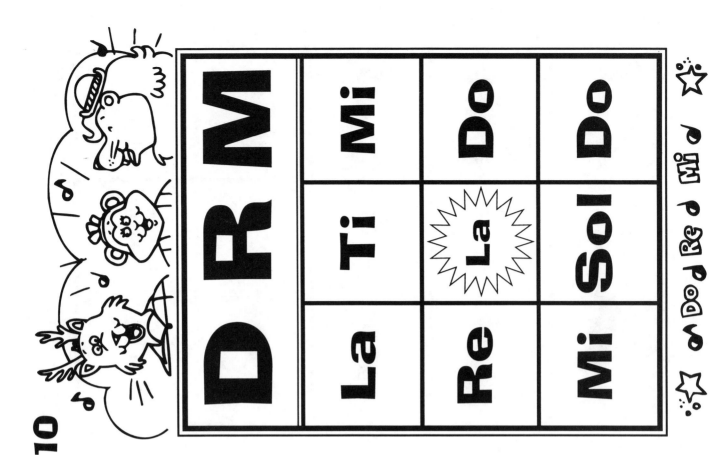

Ti	Mi	Do	Do
La	Ti	La	Sol	Do
	La	Re	Mi

9

D R M

Ti	La	Re	Do
Sol	La	Fa	Fa	Re
	Do	Fa	Re

D	R	M
Re	Sol	La
Fa	Mi	Re
Mi	Sol	Ti

D	R	M
Sol	Mi	Ti
La	Fa	Mi
Fa	La	Do

14

D R M		
La	Fa	Sol
Do	Mi	Ti
Ti	Do	Mi

Do Re Mi

13

D R M		
Fa	Mi	Re
Re	La	Mi
Ti	Re	Fa

Do Re Mi

D R M

Ti	Mi	Fa
Re	Do	Sol Ti
Do	Mi	Sol

D R M

Mi	La	La Sol
Do	Sol	Mi
Ti	Mi	La

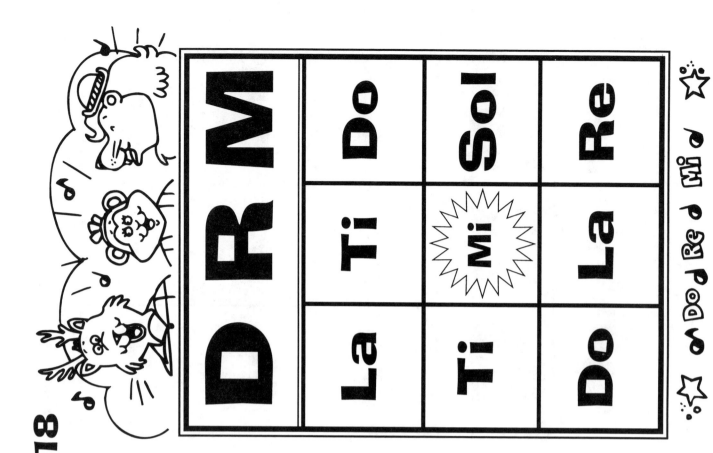

18

D R M		
Do	Ti	La
Sol	Mi	Ti
Re	La	Do

17

D R M		
Fa	Do	Ti
Mi	La	Re
Re	Fa	Fa

20

D	R	M
La	Re	Ti
Ti	Re	Fa
La	Do	Re

19

D	R	M
Sol	Fa	Mi
Re	Ti	Sol
Do	Fa	Ti Sol

♩ ♫ Do ♩ Re ♩ Mi ♩ ☆
☆ ♫ Do ♩ Re ♩ Mi ♩ ☆

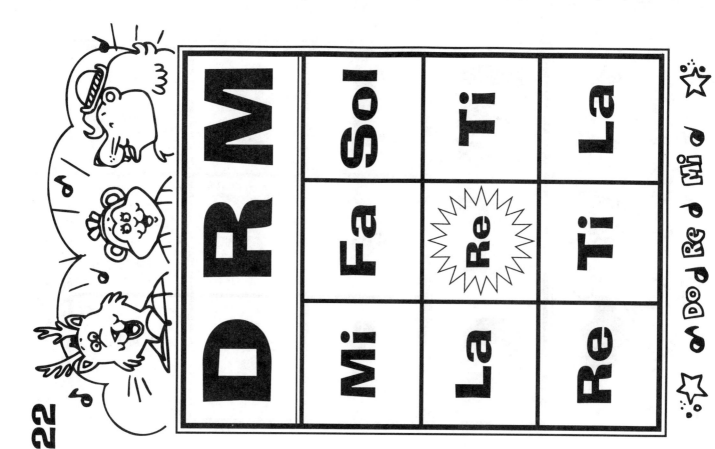

22

D R M			
	Fa Sol	Ti	La
	Mi	Re	Ti
		La	Re

☆ ♪ ♩ Do ♩ Re ♩ Mi ♩ ☆

21

D R M			
	Ti	Re	Mi
	Fa Sol	Ti	Re
	La	La	Ti

☆ ♪ ♩ Do ♩ Re ♩ Mi ♩ ☆

24

D R M		
Fa Sol	Fa	Re
Mi	Re	La
Sol Re	Ti Sol	Ti

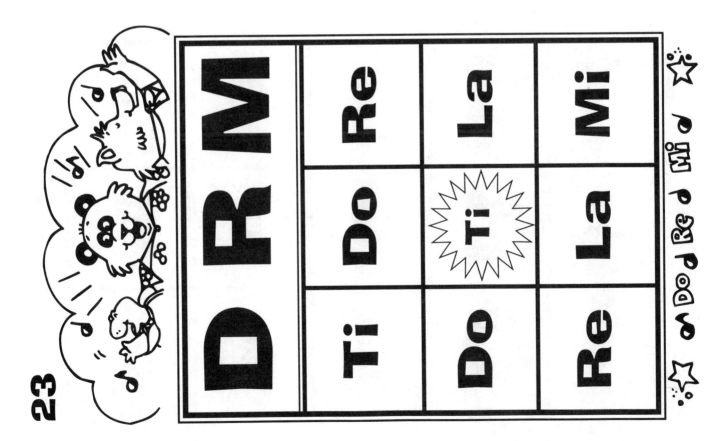

23

D R M		
Re	Do	Ti
La	Ti	Do
Mi	La	Re

DRM

Fa	La	Ti
Re	Fa	La
Do	Mi	Fa

Do Re Mi

DRM

Re	Fa	Sol
Ti	Sol	Mi
La	Re	Sol

Do Re Mi

28

D	R	M
Mi	Re	Do
Do	Sol	Re
La	Do	Mi

27

D	R	M
Fa	Mi	Re
Do	Re	Fa
Sol	Do	La

30

D	R	M
Fa	Re	Mi
La	Do	Sol
Sol	La	Do

29

D	R	M
Do	Sol	La
La	Do	Mi
Sol	Ti	Do

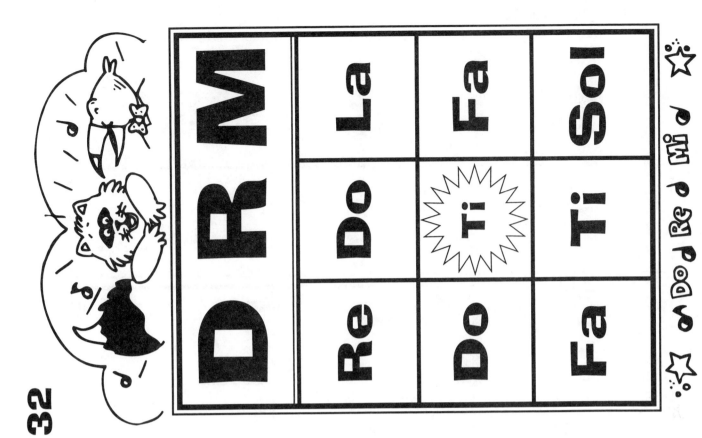

D	R	M
La	Do	Re
Fa	Ti	Do
Ti Sol	Ti	Fa

32

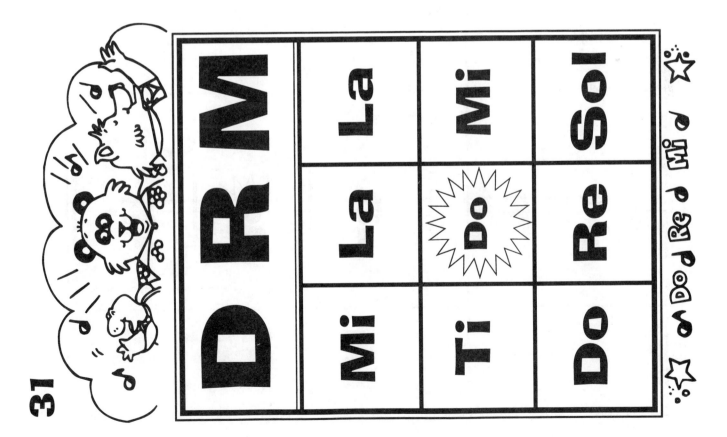

D	R	M
La	La	Mi
Mi	Do	Ti
Re Sol	Re	Do

31

D   R   M

D Do	R Do	M Do
D Re	R Re	M Re
D Mi	R Mi	M Mi
D Fa	R Fa	M Fa
D Sol	R Sol	M Sol
D La	R La	M La
D Ti	R Ti	M Ti

Do-Re-Mi Bingo Caller Cards

Musical ♪ Fingers

Musical Fingers

B

IF20453 Big Book of Music Games

IF20453 Big Book of Music Games

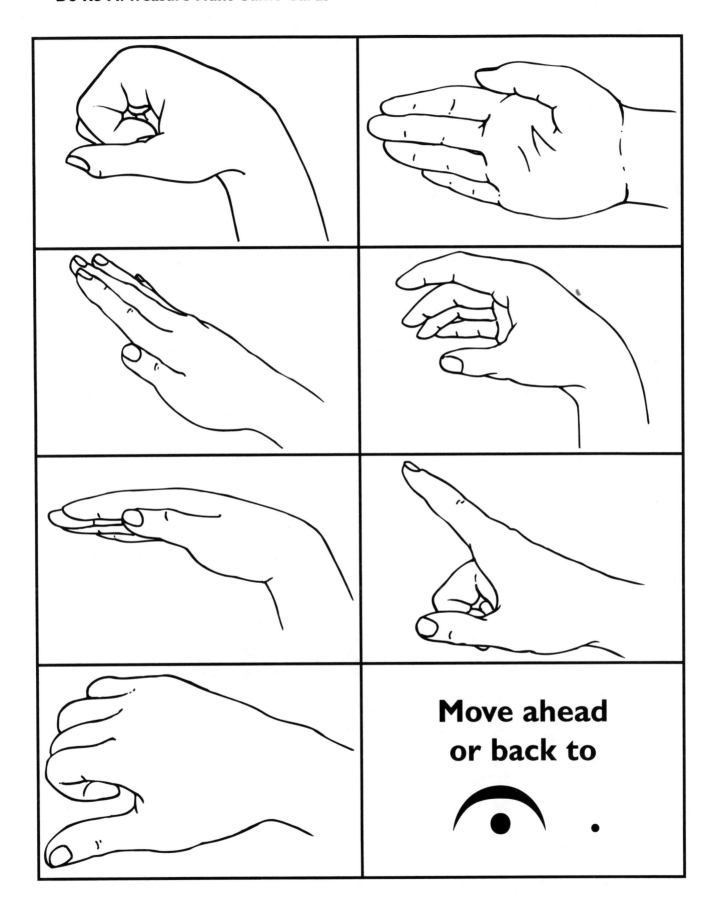

Move ahead
or back to

Take a rest!

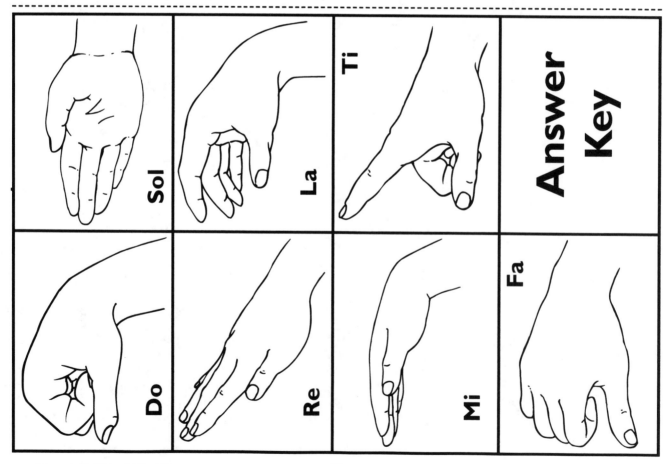

note after Do	note before La	Do not move!
note before Re	2 notes after La	2 notes before Mi
note after Mi	2 notes before Mi	Take a rest!
note before Fa	2 notes before Ti	Move to ★ !
note after Sol	2 notes after Sol	Move to ⌢• !

Seven-Up!

Notes, Rests and Reading Simple Rhythms

Notes, Rests and Reading Simple Rhythms

Symbol Presto!

Players: Teams of 5 children
Object: To identify the symbol correctly
Materials: Pattern pages 59–62, scissors, glue, construction paper

Preparation: Photocopy a set of the pattern pages for each team of children plus the "Caller." (If appropriate, print the name of the symbol on each pattern page before reproducing the cards.) Cut apart the cards. Discard the Wild Cards.

Directions: Divide the class into teams of five children. Give each team a set of cards which are distributed to the team players, three cards per player. Choose one child to be the "Caller" and one child to be the "Timer." To begin play, place the Caller's cards *face down* in a pile. The Caller draws three cards and announces the names of the symbols. If any players have those symbols, the players must hold the cards above their heads to show the Caller. This must be done within 30 seconds (or an appropriate length of time). Each team which correctly identifies the symbols within the time limit is awarded a game point. Play as many rounds as appropriate for the children.

Smart Symbols

Players: 2
Object: To correctly identify the symbols
Materials: Pattern pages 59–63, scissors, construction paper, glue, game markers, colored file folder

Preparation: Duplicate pattern page 63, mount it on a file folder and decorate as desired. Reproduce the notes and rests card patterns and mount them on construction paper. Cut apart the game cards and print the name of each symbol on the back of the card.

Directions: Mix up the game cards and place them

face down in a pile. Have each student select a game marker and place it on START. Decide if the Wild Card means a player must move ahead or back two spaces. The first player draws a game card and identifies the symbol. If the answer is correct, the player may move his or her game marker to the next space on the path. The second player takes a turn and plays in the same manner. Continue playing until one player reaches BRAVO.

Symbol Lotto

Players: 1 or more
Object: To match identical symbols or symbols with words
Materials: Pattern pages 64-65, scissors, construction paper, glue

Preparation: Reproduce the pattern pages and mount them on construction paper. Cut apart the squares on page 65.

Directions: Let the children match the game pieces.

Rollin' Rhythms

Players: 4
Object: To create appropriate rhythm patterns
Materials: Pattern pages 66–68 and 91, pencil, glue, 6 half-gallon milk cartons, scissors, plain-color adhesive plastic, clear adhesive plastic, construction paper, paper

Preparation: Obtain six clean milk cartons. To make die #1, cut off the top of two cartons at 4 inches (102 mm) from the bottom to make a cube. Trim the second carton before inserting it into the first carton. (See the illustration.) Repeat this procedure for the other two dice.

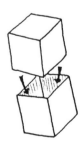

Cover the dice with plain-color adhesive plastic. Reproduce pattern pages 66–68 and then cut apart the squares. Mount the symbols on the faces of the cube. Before covering them with clear adhesive plastic, be sure to draw a red line under any symbols for clarity. Photocopy page 91, then mount the copy on construction paper. Cut apart the game cards.

Directions: For this delightful game, the children must create rhythm patterns for predetermined time signatures. To begin play, have four children form two teams of players. Place the game cards *face down* in a draw pile. For the first round, a member of the first team draws a game card. The first team continues the turn by rolling the dice. For example, if the card shows the three-four time signature and the quarter note, the players must determine which symbols shown on the dice can complete the rhythm pattern. If the pattern is finished, the team earns two points. If the dice must be rolled again, set aside the dice that show symbols that can finish the pattern and then roll the remaining die (dice). If the team is able to finish the pattern on the second roll, the team earns one point. If the team is unable to finish the pattern, the team scores no points. The other team continues the first round of play in the same manner. Continue the game until all game cards have been used. The team with the most points wins.

Variation: Have the players use the game cards on page 88 and create corresponding rhythm patterns. Be sure to discard the cards "Mark any space."

Notes 'n' Cash

Players: 2 or 3
Object: To collect the most cash
Materials: Pattern pages 69–71, scissors, glue, construction paper, tape, tagboard, large envelope, clear adhesive tape, optional: blank dice, classroom money

Preparation: Photocopy the game chart on page 70 and mount it on construction paper. To prepare the dice, photocopy page 71, then mount it on tagboard. Cut out the dice patterns. Fold on the dashed lines and tape the edges to form each cube. (If you prefer, pur-

chase two blank dice and print the symbols on them.) Reproduce 16 or more copies of pages 69 and 71 for the money game pieces. Mount the money on construction paper and then cut apart the coins and bills. Store the items in a large envelope. If available, provide $1 and $5 bills and half-dollars from a classroom money set.

Directions: This game will certainly be a favorite in your classroom. Set the materials on a tabletop. Decide which player starts the game. The first player rolls the dice, locates the symbols on the chart, and collects the corresponding amount of money. The second player continues in the same manner. Continue the game until one player has collected a certain amount of money or for a predetermined amount of time or number of turns. The player with the most money is the winner.

Blackout Bingo

Players: 5 or 6
Object: The first player to cover all spaces on her or his board is the winner.
Materials: Pattern pages 72–77, scissors, construction paper, game markers, glue

Preparation: Photocopy the bingo card patterns and mount them on construction paper. Duplicate a copy of pattern page 77, then cut apart the cards.

Directions: Have each player select a bingo board. If appropriate, ask one student to be the "Caller." To begin play, the Caller draws a card and announces the symbol. Each player marks the corresponding space on his or her bingo board. Continue playing in this manner until someone covers all spaces for "Blackout Bingo."

Notable Toss

Players: 2
Object: The first player to cover 10 tambourines on the board is the winner.
Materials: Pattern pages 78-79, scissors, glue, watercolor markers, colored file folder, game markers

Preparation: Use the dice from "Notes 'n' Cash" or make an additional set. Photocopy the game board pattern pages and mount them on a file folder. Color the game board if desired.

Directions: Each player chooses a panel on the game board. Have the players take turns rolling the dice, identifying the symbols, and covering the corresponding spaces. If the symbols are already covered, the player loses that turn. Continue playing until one player has covered 10 tambourines. Play again. Encourage the players to keep track of who wins each time.

Catch the Beat!

Players: 2
Object: To correctly identify three-four and four-four meters
Materials: Pattern pages 80-81, scissors, glue, colored file folder, game markers, pencil, paper clip

Preparation: Photocopy the game board pattern pages and mount them on a file folder. Color the game board if desired.

Directions: The players must think carefully about the rhythm patterns shown on the maracas. The pattern is either in three-four or four-four meter. Each player selects a panel on the game board. To begin play, the first player uses a pencil and paper clip to spin the dial. (Refer to page 7 for additional instructions.) The first player finishes her or his turn by marking the corresponding rhythm pattern. The second player continues in the same manner. When all the maracas have been marked on a panel, the game ends.

Think and Match!

Players: 6 or less
Object: To identify two-four, three-four, four-four, and six-eight meters
Materials: Pattern pages 82–89, construction paper, glue, scissors, watercolor markers, game markers

Preparation: Photocopy pattern pages 82–88 and mount them on construction paper. Color the game boards if desired. Cut apart the cards on page 88 for the "Caller." Set aside the answer key provided on page 89 for later use.

Directions: Choose one player to be the Caller. Each player selects a game board. Mix up the game cards and place them *face down* in a pile. The Caller draws a card and reads the meter. Each player marks the corresponding rhythm pattern. If the pattern is already marked, the player loses that turn. Continue playing in this manner until one player has marked all spaces on his or her game board. If necessary, use the answer key on page 89 to check the players' work.

Variation: For a "Rhythm Rap" activity, duplicate several copies of the pattern pages and cut apart the individual boxes to make sets of game cards. Give each team of four children a set of cards plus a copy of page 90. Have each team sort the cards according to the meter and then arrange them into long rhythm patterns. Encourage the children to clap/tap the new patterns or "Rhythm Raps."

Notes and Rests Memory Match

Players: 2 or more
Object: To collect the most pairs of cards
Materials: Pattern pages 92-93, scissors, construction paper, glue, markers

Preparation and Directions: See "Music Alphabet Memory Match" on page 6.

Note-Tac-Toe

Players: 2
Object: To cover 3 spaces in a row
Materials: Pattern page 94, game markers

Preparation: Duplicate the pattern page.

Directions: The players take turns identifying a note or rest and then marking the space. The first player to mark three spaces in a row is the winner.

Notes Card Patterns

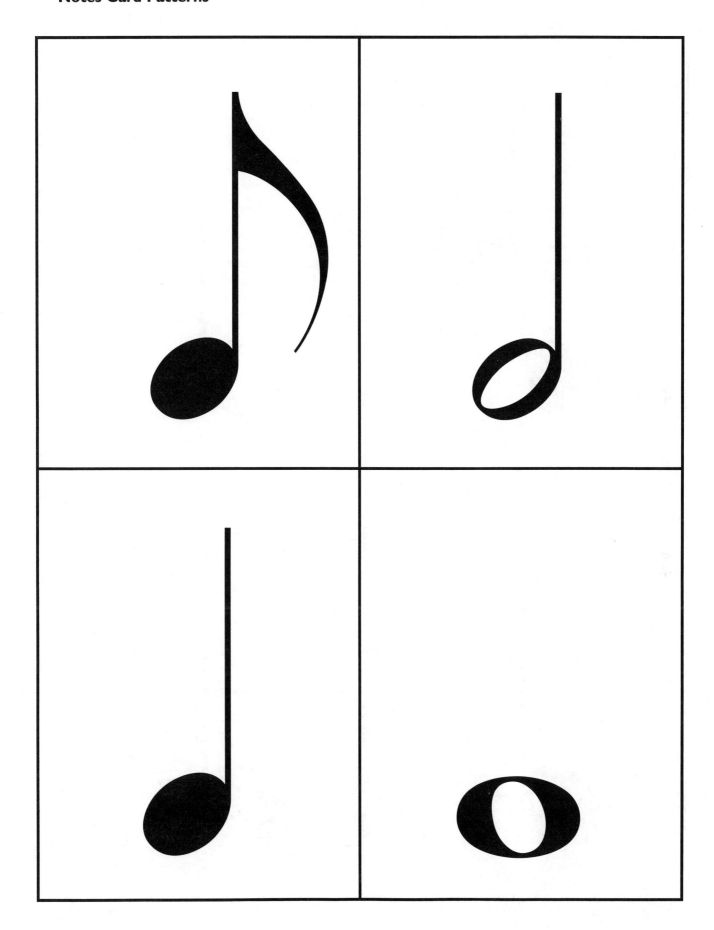

Rests Card Patterns

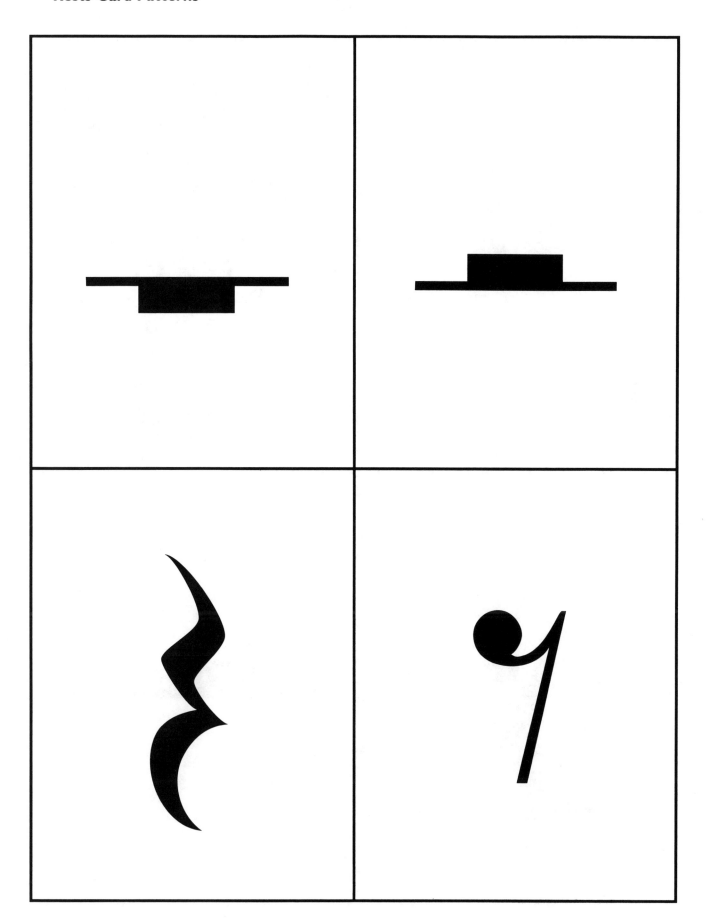

Rests Card Patterns

Bravo!

Smart Symbols

Start

Symbol Lotto

Symbol Lotto

quarter note	whole note	half note
eighth note	quarter rest	whole rest
half rest	eighth rest	dotted quarter note
dotted half note	sixteenth rest	sixteenth note

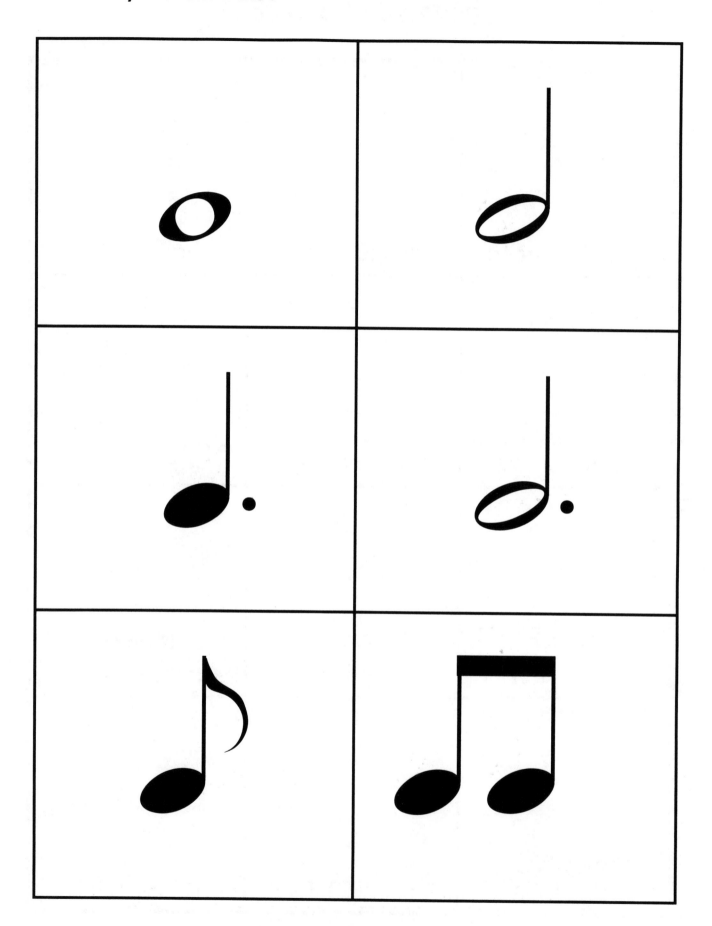

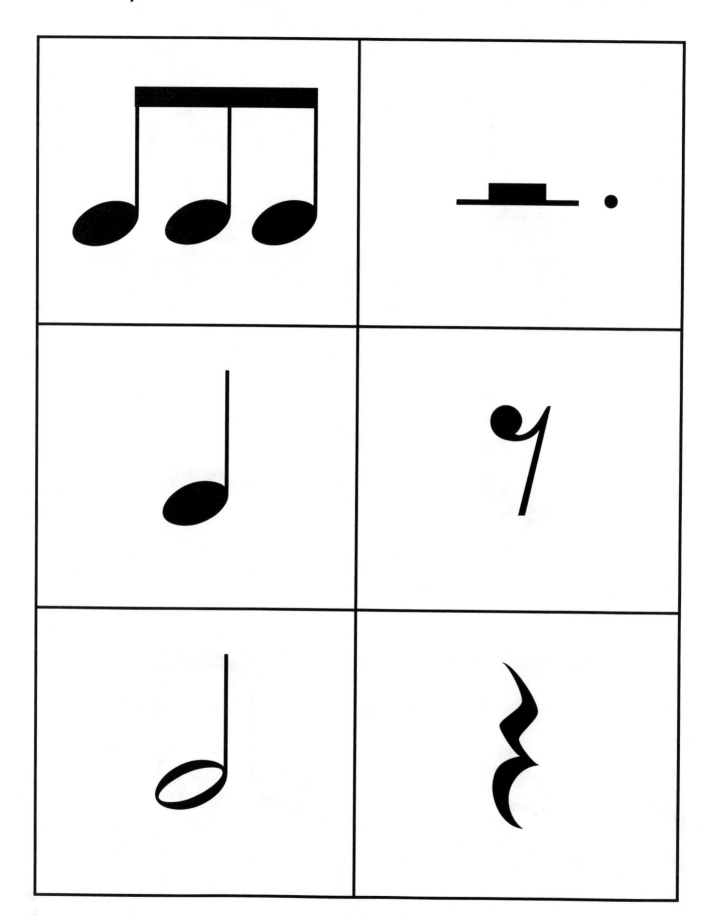

Notes 'n' Cash Patterns

Notes 'n' Cash

	Eighth Rest- ½ beat ♪	Quarter Rest- 1 beat 𝄽	Dotted Quarter Note- 1½ beat 𝄽·	Half Rest- 2 beats ▬	Dotted Half Rest- 3 beats ▬·	Whole Rest- 4 beats ▬
Eighth Note- ½ beat ♪	1	1½	2	2½	3½	4½
Quarter Note- 1 beat ♩	1½	2	2½	3	4	5
Dotted Quarter Note- 1½ beats ♩·	2	2½	3	3½	4½	5½
Half Note- 2 beats ♩	2½	3	3½	4	5	6
Dotted Half Note- 3 beats ♩·	3½	4	4½	5	6	7
Whole Note- 4 beats 𝅝	4½	5	5½	6	7	8

Notes 'n' Cash Patterns

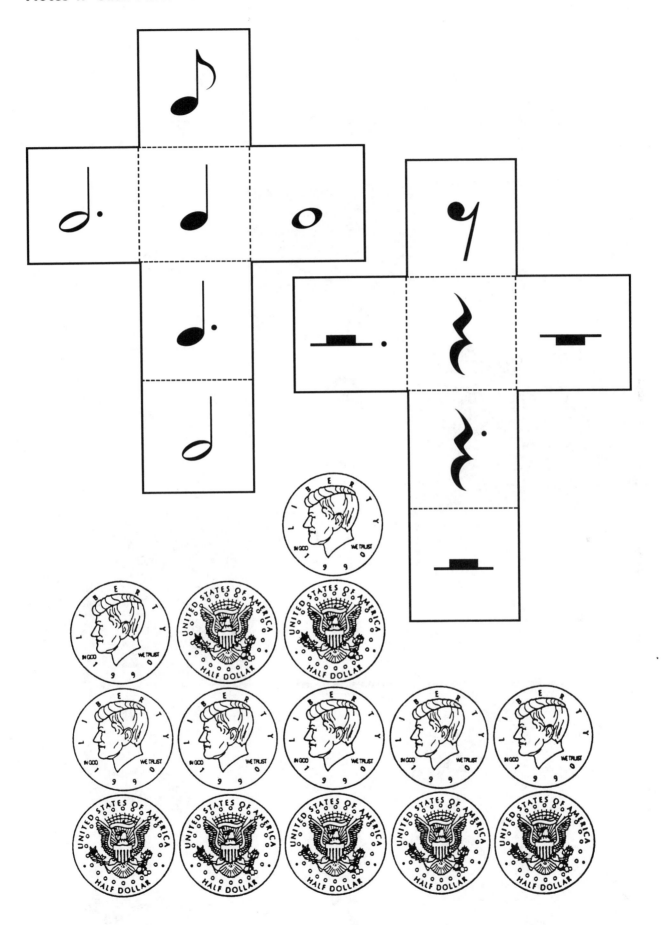

71

Notes and Rests
Blackout Bingo

Notes and Rests
Blackout Bingo

IF20453 *Big Book of Music Games*

Notes and Rests
Blackout Bingo

Notes and Rests
Blackout Bingo

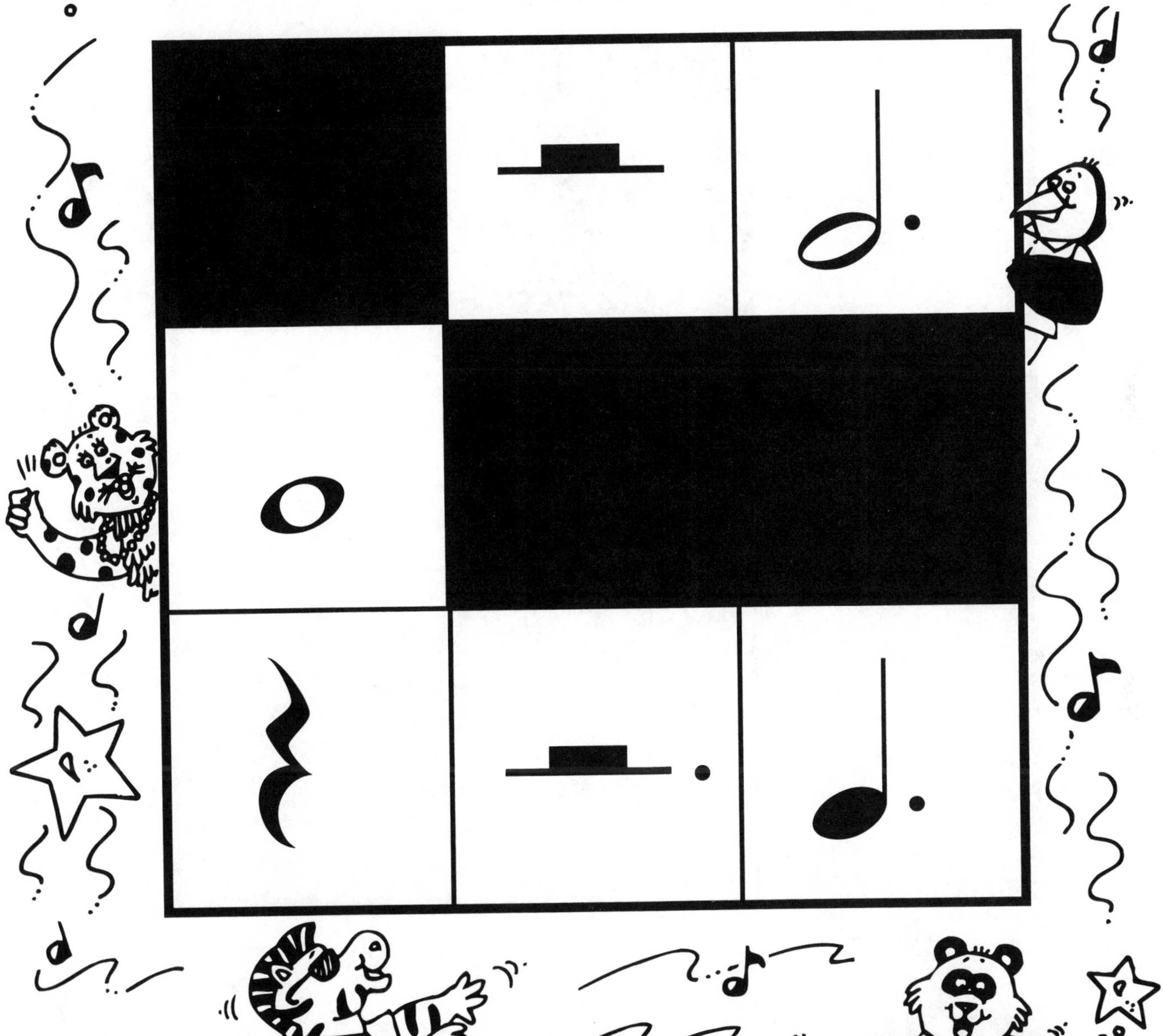

5

Notes and Rests
Blackout Bingo

Blackout Bingo Caller Cards

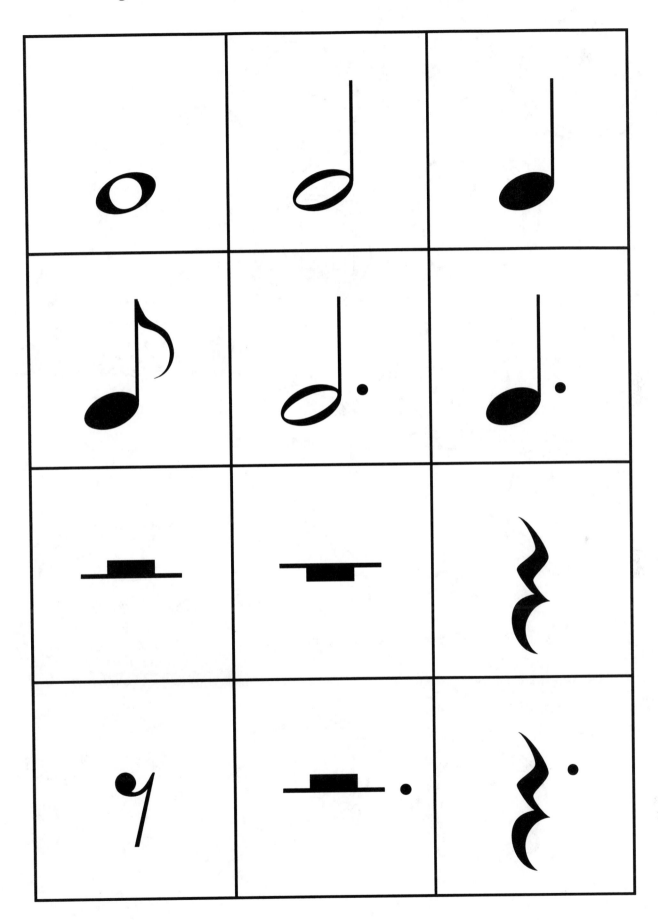

Catch the Beat!

Think and match!

Think and match!

3

Think and match!

Think and match!

Think and match!

Think and match!

$\frac{2}{4}$	$\frac{2}{4}$	$\frac{2}{4}$	$\frac{2}{4}$
$\frac{3}{4}$	$\frac{3}{4}$	$\frac{3}{4}$	$\frac{3}{4}$
$\frac{3}{4}$	$\frac{4}{4}$	$\frac{4}{4}$	$\frac{4}{4}$
$\frac{4}{4}$	$\frac{4}{4}$	$\frac{4}{4}$	$\frac{6}{8}$
$\frac{6}{8}$	$\frac{6}{8}$	Mark Any Space.	Mark Any Space.

Think and Match Answer Key

1

$\frac{3}{4}$	$\frac{2}{4}$
$\frac{4}{4}$	$\frac{4}{4}$
$\frac{3}{4}$	$\frac{6}{8}$

2

$\frac{6}{8}$	$\frac{4}{4}$
$\frac{3}{4}$	$\frac{2}{4}$
$\frac{4}{4}$	$\frac{3}{4}$

3

$\frac{3}{4}$	$\frac{2}{4}$
$\frac{6}{8}$	$\frac{4}{4}$
$\frac{4}{4}$	$\frac{3}{4}$

4

$\frac{6}{8}$	$\frac{2}{4}$
$\frac{3}{4}$	$\frac{3}{4}$
$\frac{2}{4}$	$\frac{4}{4}$

5

$\frac{3}{4}$	$\frac{6}{8}$
$\frac{2}{4}$	$\frac{4}{4}$
$\frac{2}{4}$	$\frac{6}{8}$

6

$\frac{2}{4}$	$\frac{6}{8}$
$\frac{6}{8}$	$\frac{3}{4}$
$\frac{4}{4}$	$\frac{4}{4}$

Rhythm Rap Cards

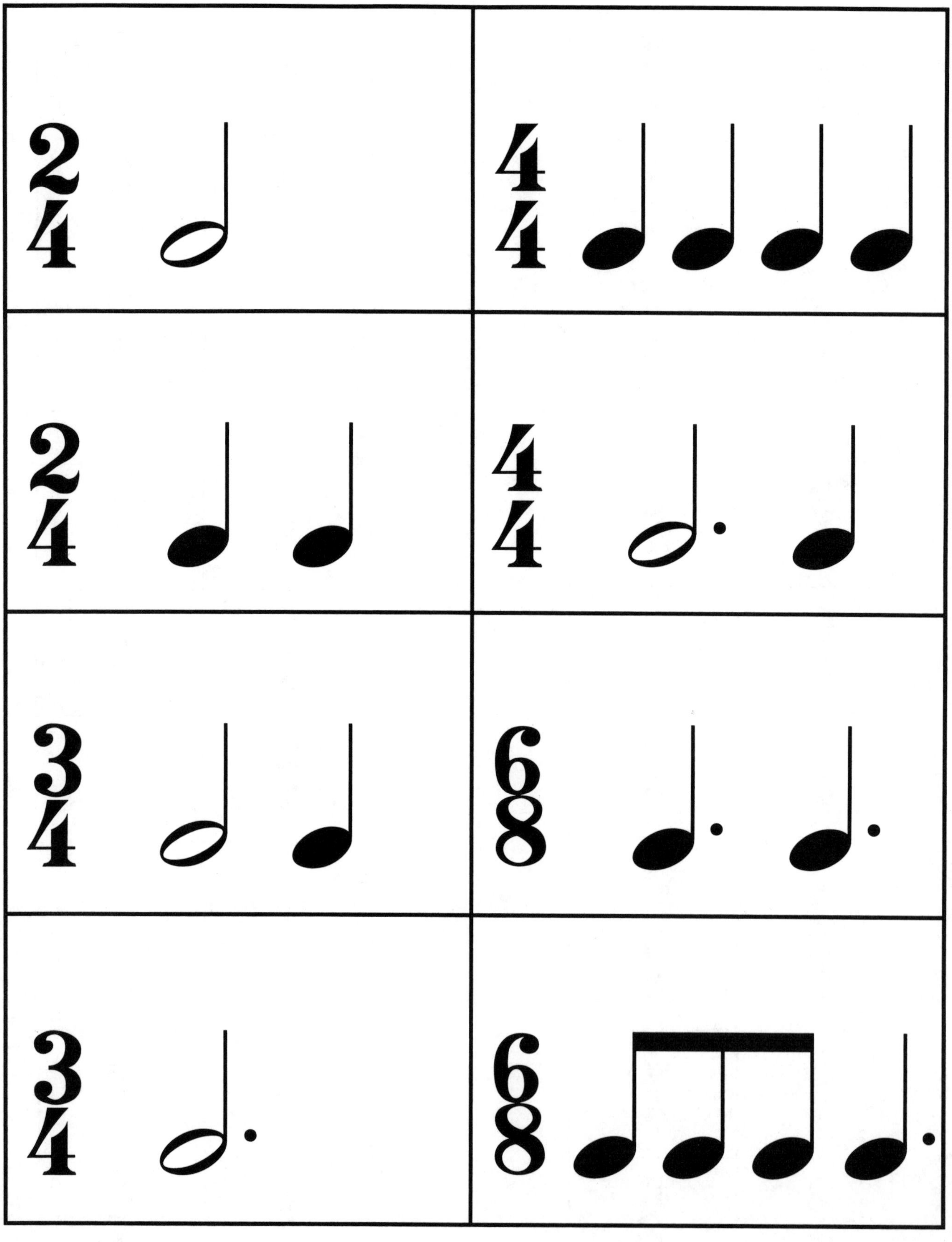

Rhythm Starter Cards

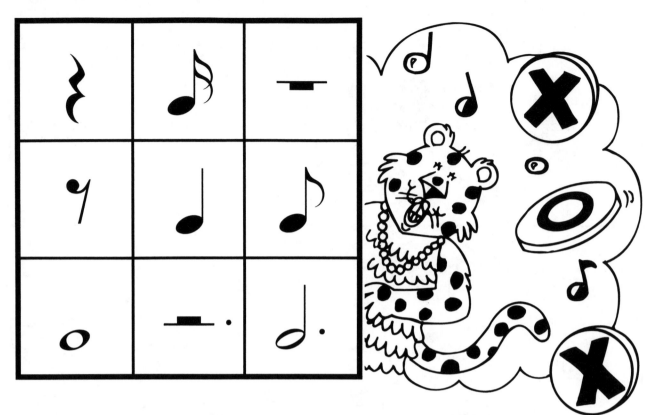

NOTE-TAC-TOE

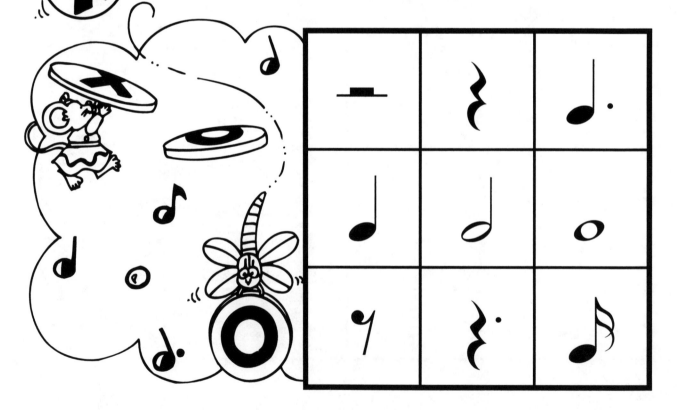

More
Music Symbols

More Music Symbols

More Symbols Presto!

Players: Teams of 5 children
Object: To identify the symbol correctly
Materials: Pattern pages 98–104, scissors, glue, construction paper

Preparation: Follow the same procedure used for "Symbol Presto!" on page 56.

Directions: Play the game in the same manner as "Symbol Presto!"

Symbol-Tac-Toe

Players: 2
Object: To cover 3 spaces in a row
Materials: Pattern page 105, construction paper, glue, game markers

Preparation: Duplicate the pattern page and mount it on construction paper.

Directions: Give each player a set of game markers. The players take turns identifying a symbol and then marking the space. The first player to mark three spaces in a vertical, horizontal, or diagonal row is the winner. If the players are interested, have them use both grids during the game. When finished with a game, invite the children to play again and keep track of who wins each time or if the game ends in a tie.

More Symbol Lotto

Players: 6 or less
Object: To correctly match symbols with words
Materials: Pattern pages 107–114, scissors, construction paper, glue, watercolor markers, large envelope

Preparation: Duplicate the pattern pages and mount them on construction paper. Decorate the game boards if desired. Cut apart the game cards on pages 112–114. When finished, store the game pieces in a large envelope.

Directions: Have the children sit in a large circle. Place the game cards *face down* in the center. Mix up the cards. Let each child select a game board. To begin play, the first player draws a card and matches it with the corresponding symbol or term. If a match cannot be made, the player loses that turn and returns the game card to the draw pile. If a match is made, the card is placed in the corresponding space on the player's board. The second player takes a turn to find a match. Continue the game in this manner until one player has filled his or her game board with corresponding cards.

Call It! Symbols and Terms

Players: 34 or less
Object: To answer all the clues as a team within a specified time
Materials: Pattern pages 115–131, construction paper/tagboard, glue, scissors, laminating material

Preparation: Photocopy the pattern pages and mount them on construction paper or tagboard. Cut apart the game cards. Laminate them if desired.

Directions: This fast action game (a round robin game) will certainly entertain the students in your class. Each player will have an opportunity to answer a clue and read a new clue. The class must work as a team to finish the game within a predetermined length of time.

Distribute the cards to the students. If there are extra cards, encourage some students to select two cards. As a class, decide what the time limit will be. (It may be appropriate to play a trial game before deciding on a

time limit.) To start the game, the player who holds the "treble clef" game card reads the first clue. All players check their cards to find the answer. The player who holds the correct symbol announces the answer and shows the card. This player reads out loud a different clue which is printed on the bottom of her or his card. Another player with the correct answer shows his or her card and then quickly reads the next clue. Continue the game in this manner until all players have answered clues. If the game is completed within the time limit, the class wins the game.

Symbol Bingo

Players: Entire class
Object: The first player to cover 5 spaces in a row is the winner.
Materials: Pattern pages 132–163, scissors, construction paper, game markers, glue

Preparation: Photocopy the bingo card patterns (30 cards in set). Mount the copies on construction paper. Duplicate two copies of pattern pages 162-163. Cut apart one copy to make the game cards for the "Caller."

Directions: If appropriate, ask one student to be the Caller. To begin play, have the Caller draw a card and then announce the symbol/term shown on the card. Each player marks the corresponding space on her or his bingo board. Continue playing in this manner until someone covers five spaces in a vertical, horizontal, or diagonal row.

Variation: Perhaps the students are interested in covering the bingo boards in different formats. Be creative and make some suggestions for the students to use when playing this game.

Baseball Forte

Players: 2 teams of 3 or more players
Object: To correctly identify the symbols to score points for the team
Materials: Pattern pages 164–168, colored file folder, construction paper, glue, scissors, pencils, game markers, watercolor markers

Preparation: Reproduce the pattern pages and color the game board if desired. Mount pages 164-165 on a file folder. Glue the game cards to construction paper and then cut them apart. Duplicate several copies of the score sheet (see page 168).

Directions: For this entertaining game, let the students form teams of three or more players. To begin the first inning, decide which team starts the game. Have a player on the opposing team draw a card and read the challenge. The first "batter" must answer the challenge by locating the corresponding symbol on the playing field. If the answer is correct, the player moves his or her team marker accordingly: "single"–one base, "double"–two bases, "triple"–three bases, or "home run"–return to home plate. During the inning, allow only one "out" or incorrect answer. When this happens, have the team record the score and allow the other team to be the "batters." Continue playing for nine innings. The team with the higher score is the winner.

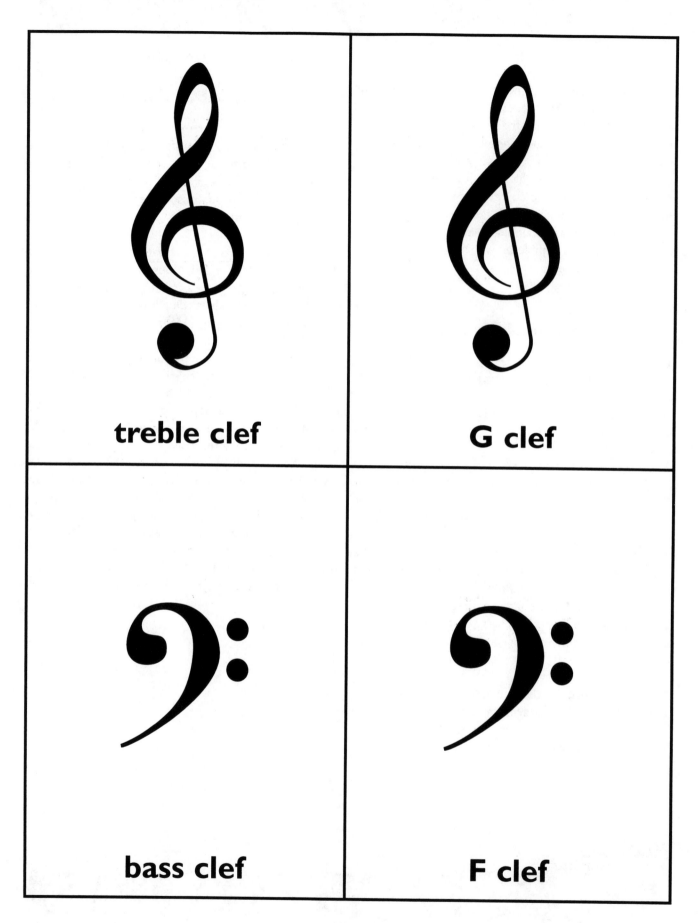

treble clef

G clef

bass clef

F clef

p

piano

pp

pianissimo

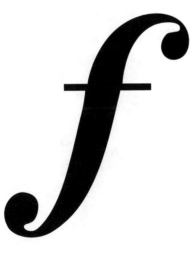

forte

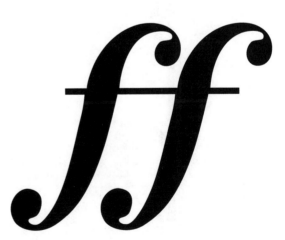

fortissimo

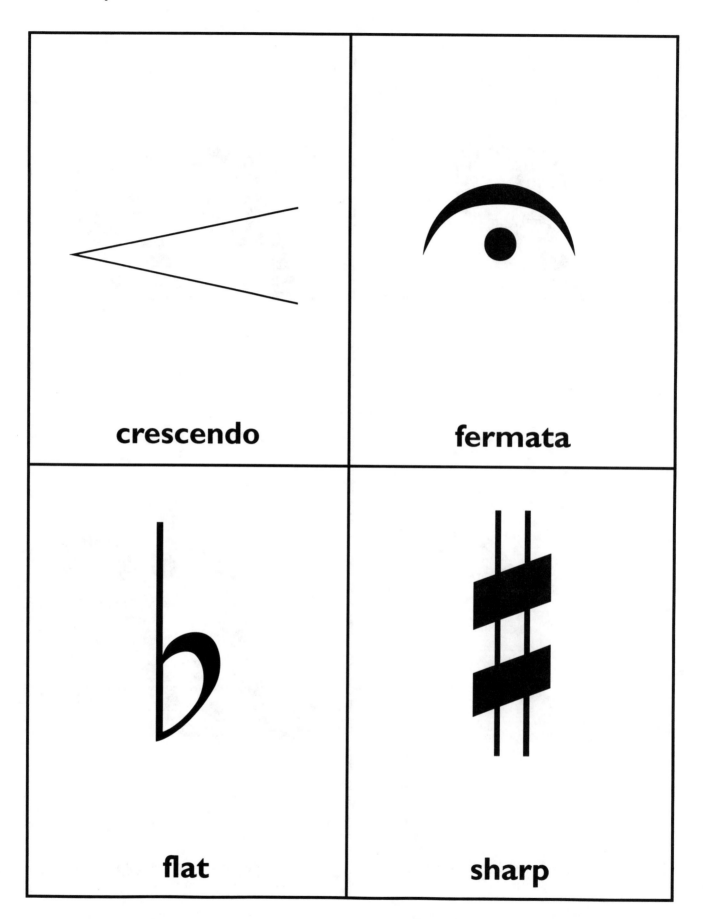

crescendo

fermata

flat

sharp

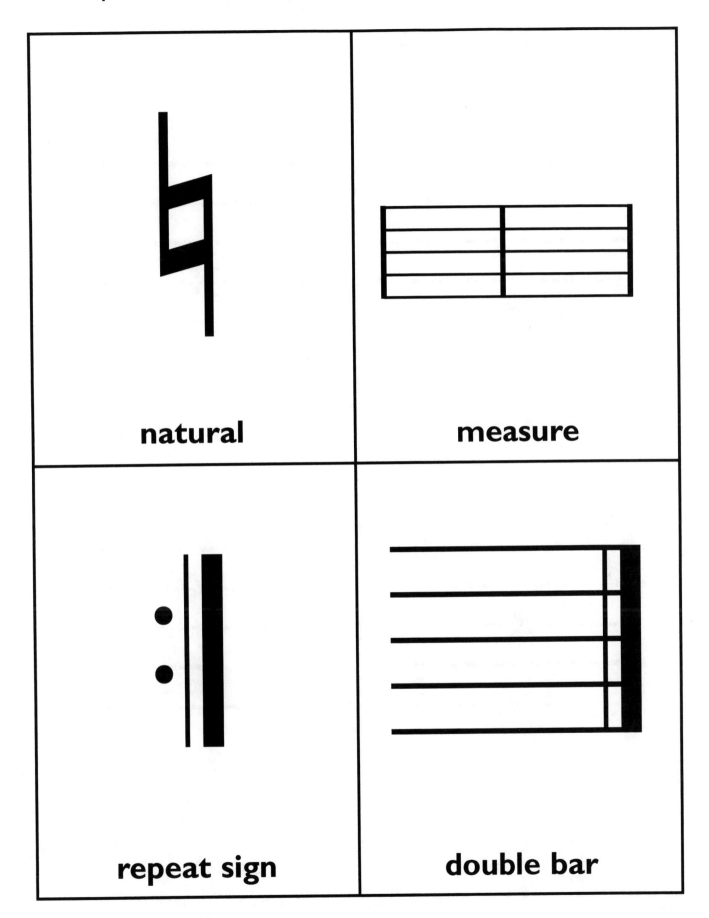

natural

measure

repeat sign

double bar

More Symbols Card Patterns

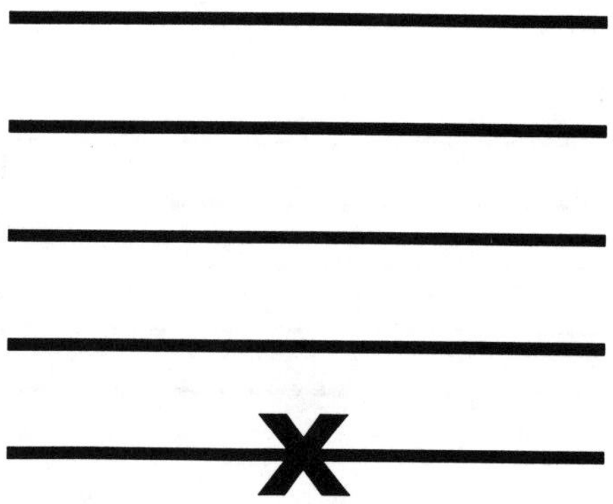

first line

second line

third line

fourth line

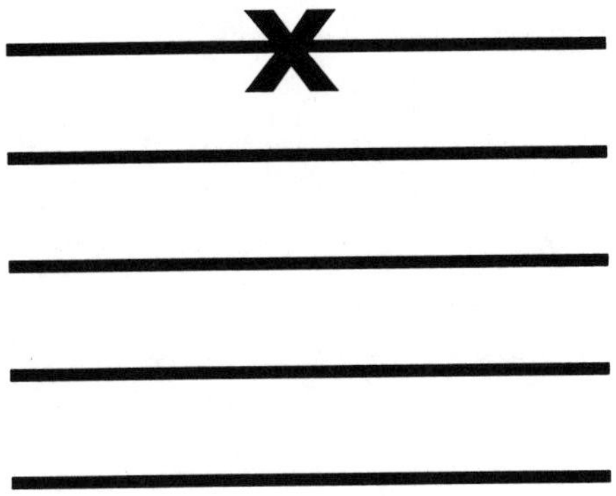

fifth line

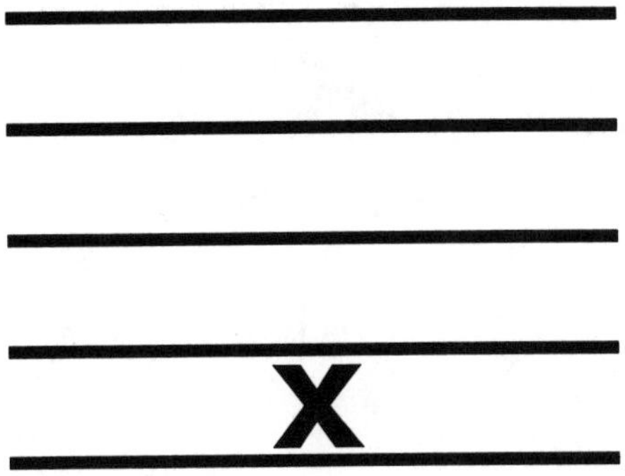

first space

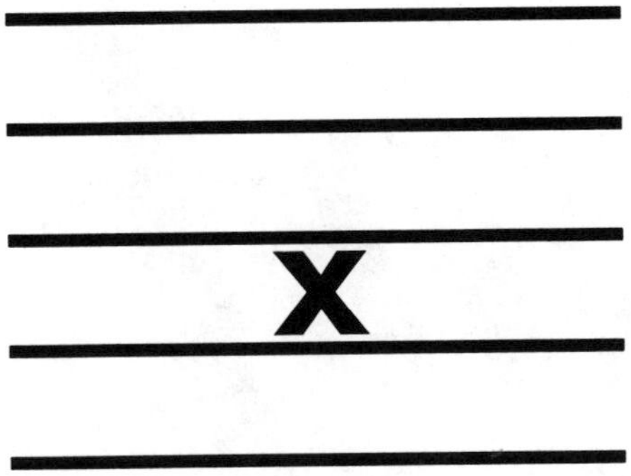

second space

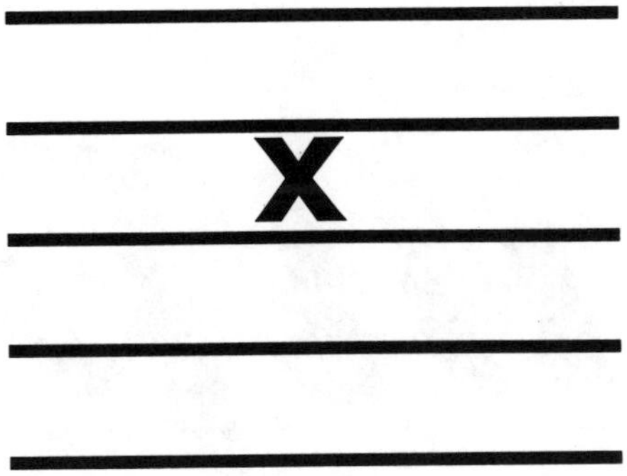

third space

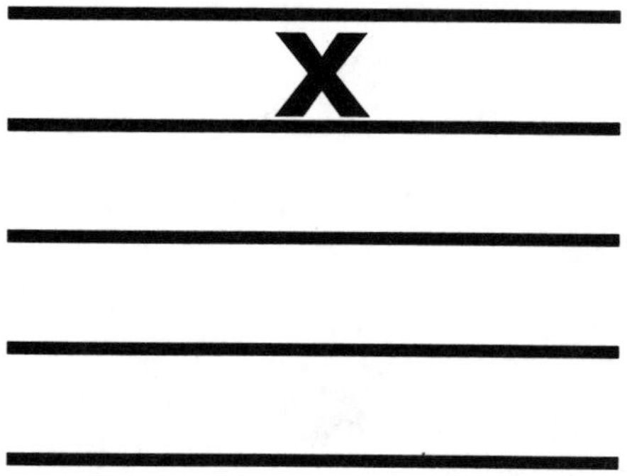

fourth space

staff

mp

mezzo piano

mf

mezzo forte

SYMBOL-TAC-TOE

Symbol Lotto

	fourth space	F clef

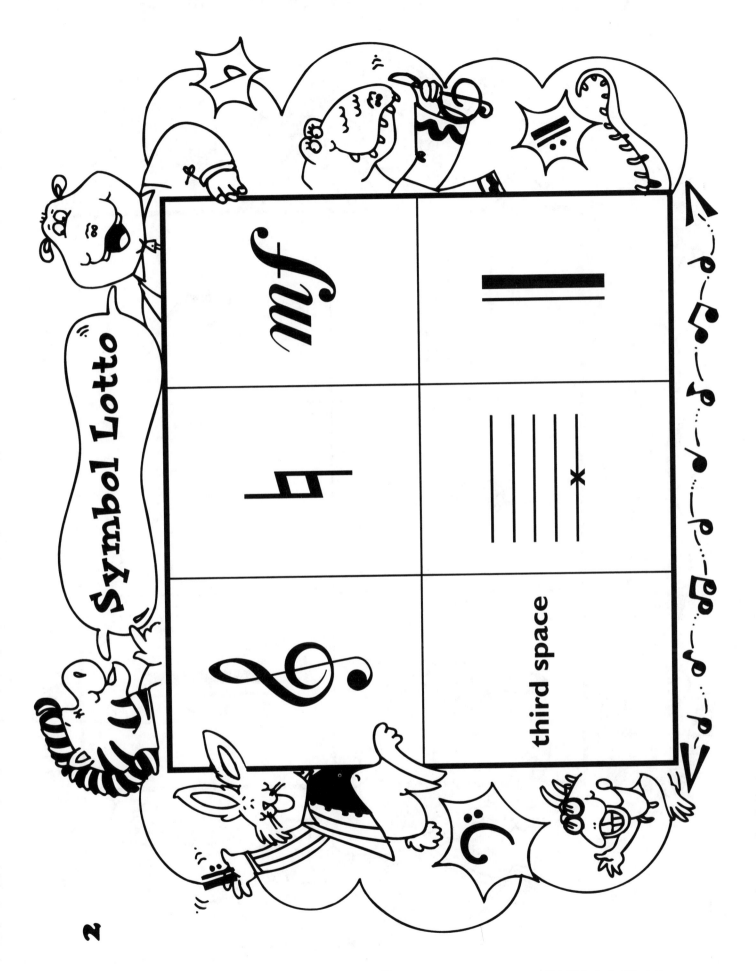

Symbol Lotto

mf

third space

2

Symbol Lotto

first space

Symbol Lotto

(staff lines with x)	f
treble clef	third line
♭	(crescendo symbol)

4

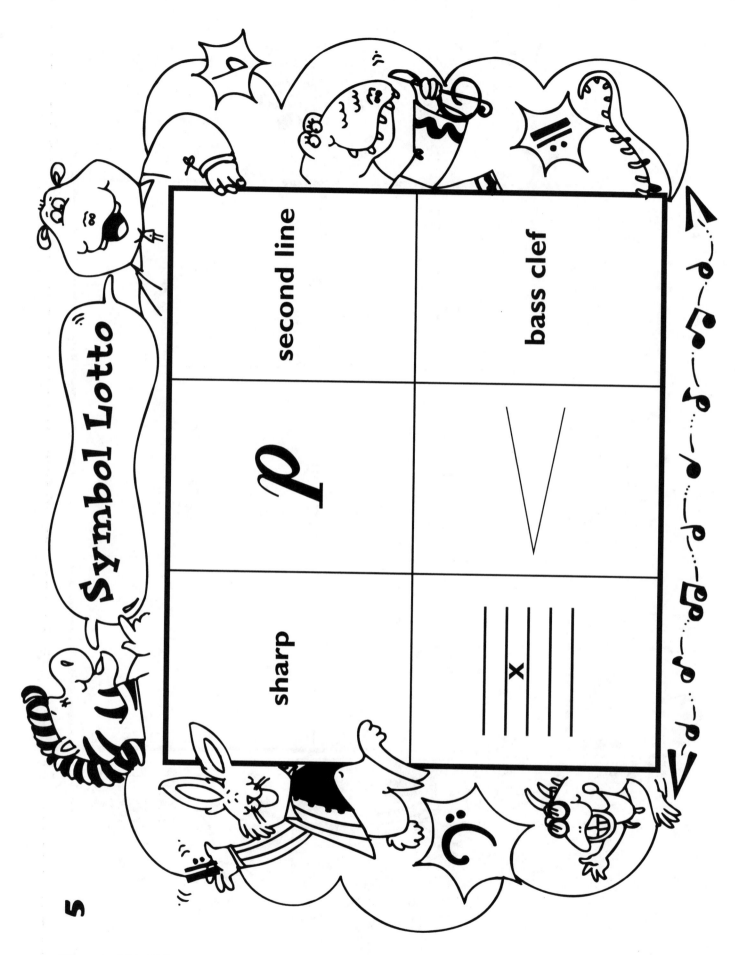

Symbol Lotto

second line	p	sharp
bass clef	V	(staff with x)

5

Symbol Lotto

G clef		flat
fifth line	*mp*	x

staff	fermata	piano
decrescendo	repeat sign	mezzo forte
second space	third space	fourth line
first line	third line	fourth space

	treble clef	bass clef

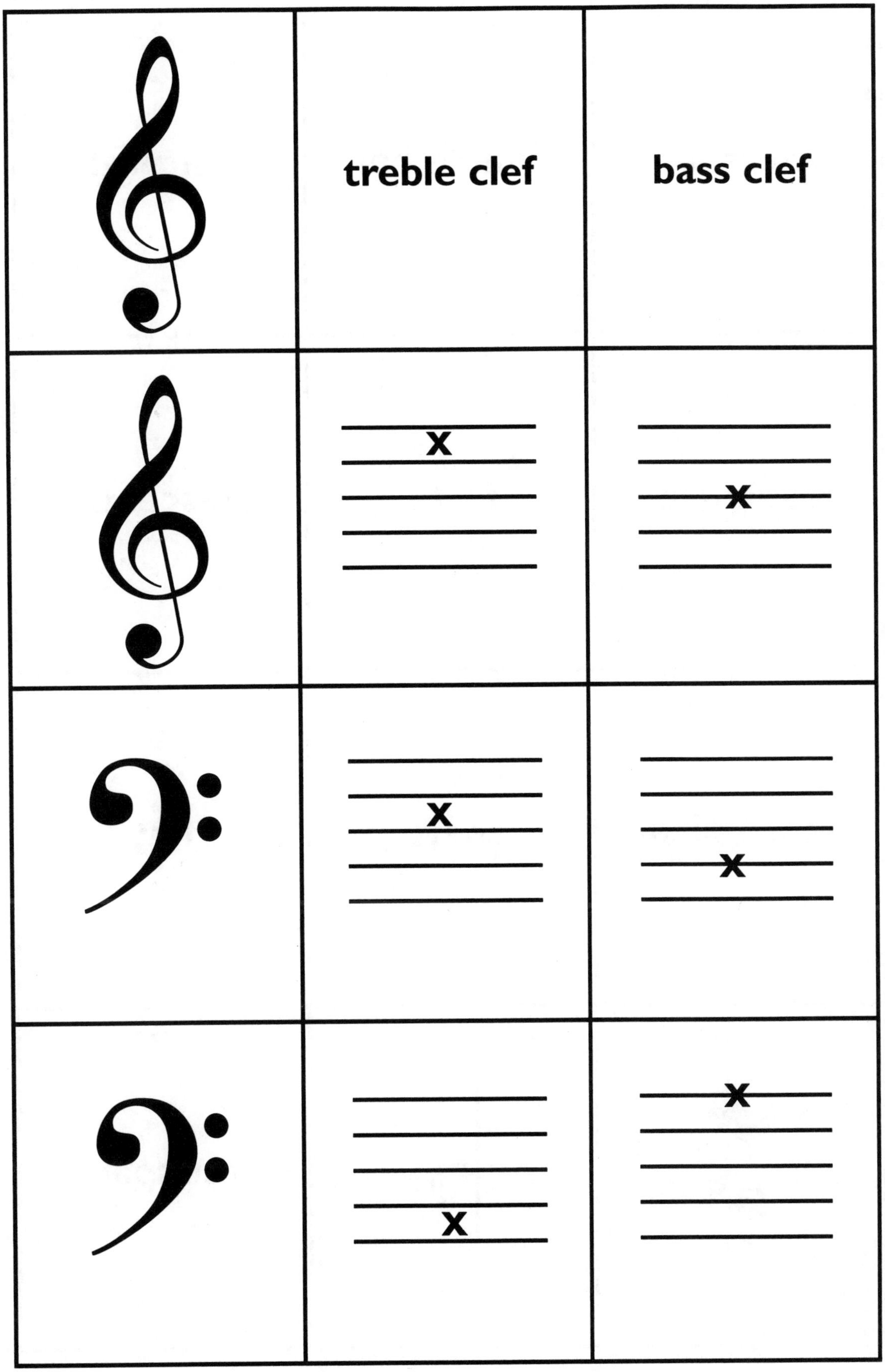

measure	double bar	natural
treble clef	forte	crescendo
mezzo piano	sharp	flat
♯	♭	first space

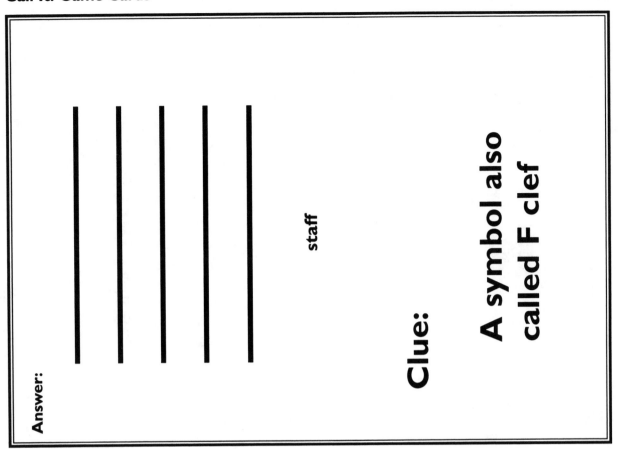

Answer:

staff

Clue:

A symbol also called F clef

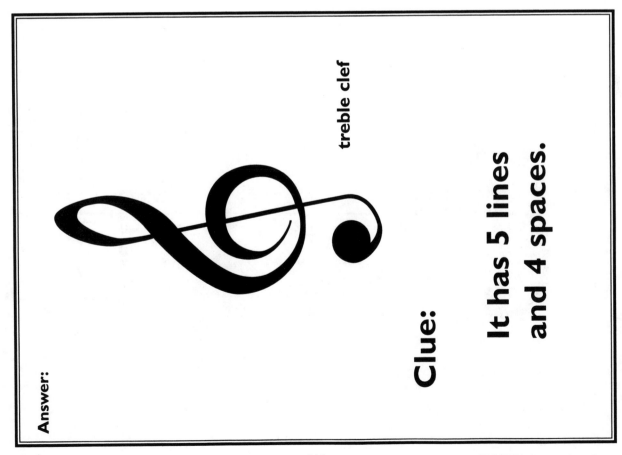

Answer:

treble clef

Clue:

It has 5 lines and 4 spaces.

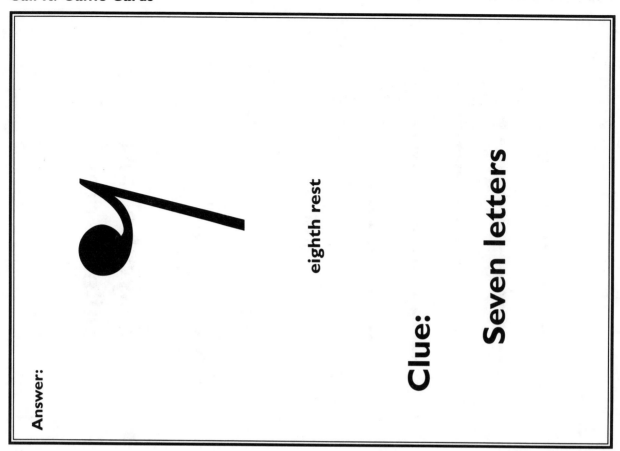

Answer:

eighth rest

Clue:

Seven letters

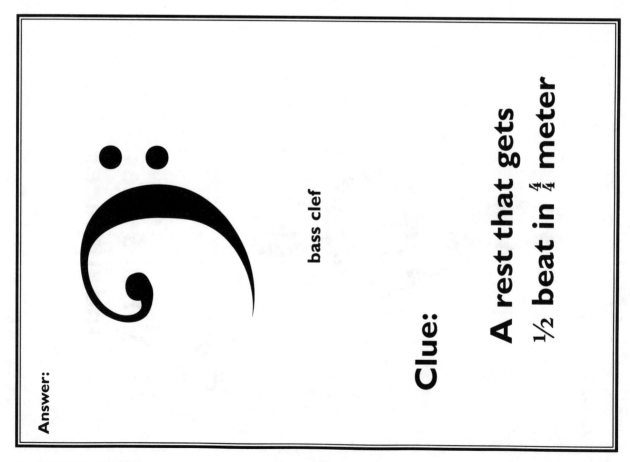

Answer:

bass clef

Clue:

A rest that gets ½ beat in $\frac{4}{4}$ meter

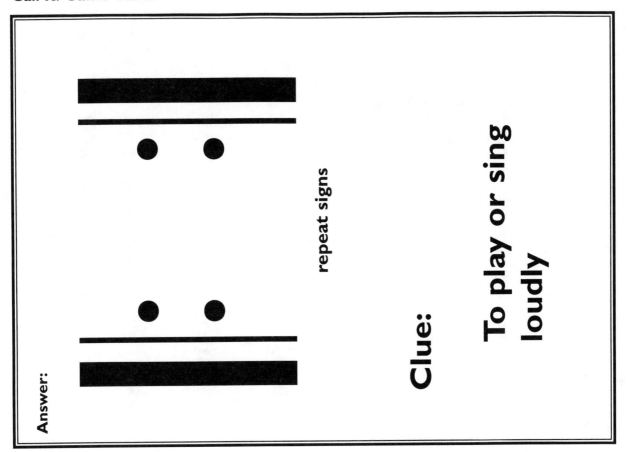

Answer:

repeat signs

Clue:

To play or sing loudly

Answer:

music alphabet

Clue:

To sing or play a section again

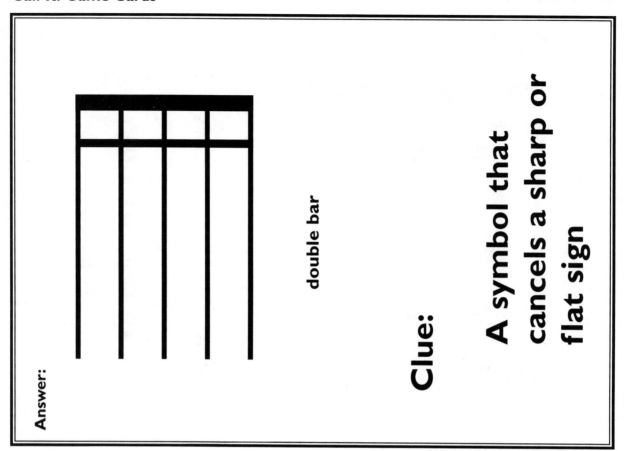

Answer:

double bar

Clue:

A symbol that cancels a sharp or flat sign

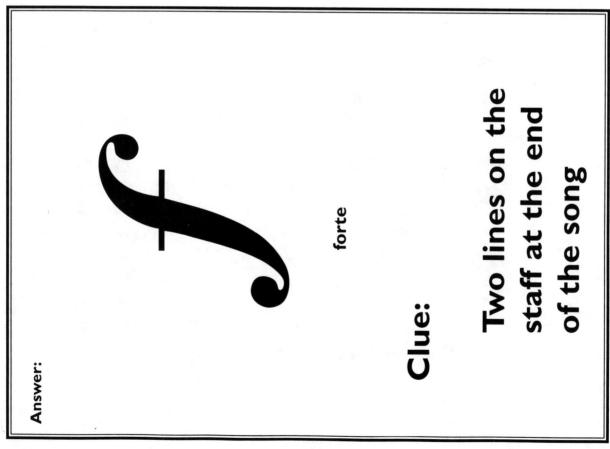

Answer:

forte

Clue:

Two lines on the staff at the end of the song

Answer:

Clue:

**The second space
on a staff**

fermata

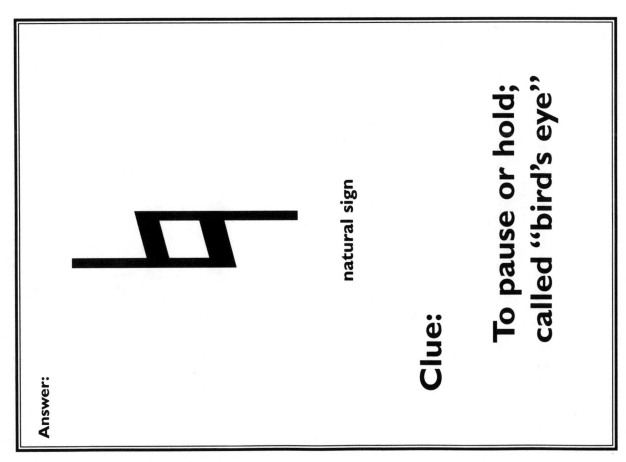

Answer:

Clue:

**To pause or hold;
called "bird's eye"**

natural sign

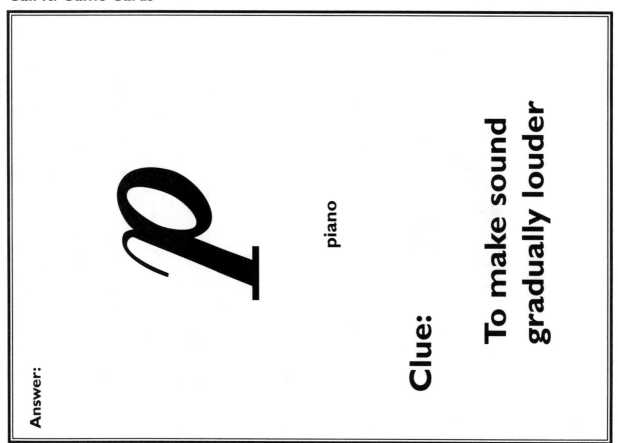

Answer:

piano

Clue:

To make sound gradually louder

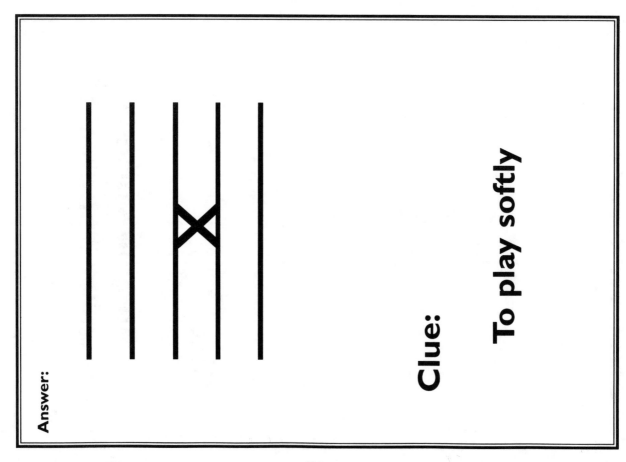

Answer:

Clue:

To play softly

Answer:

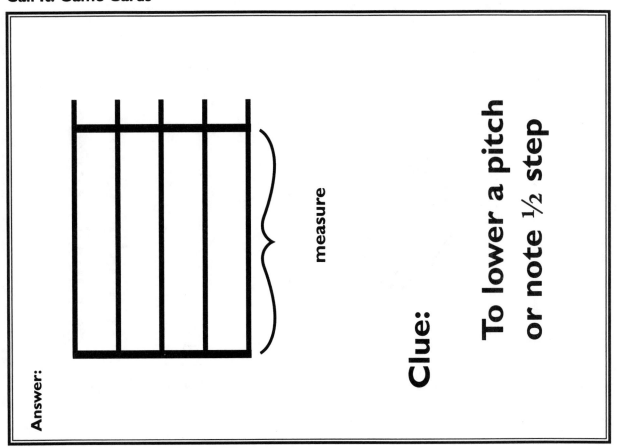

measure

Clue:

To lower a pitch or note ½ step

Answer:

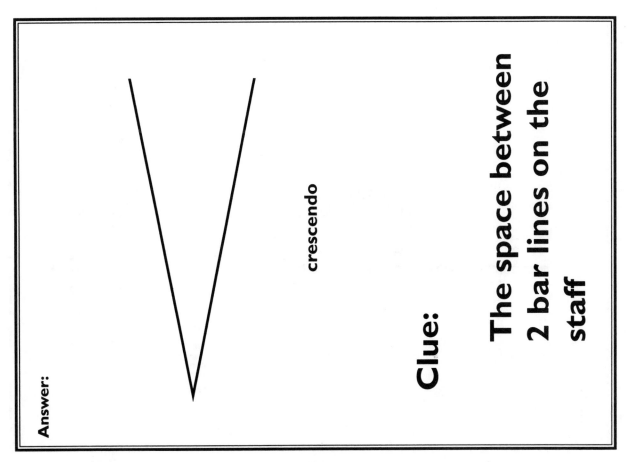

crescendo

Clue:

The space between 2 bar lines on the staff

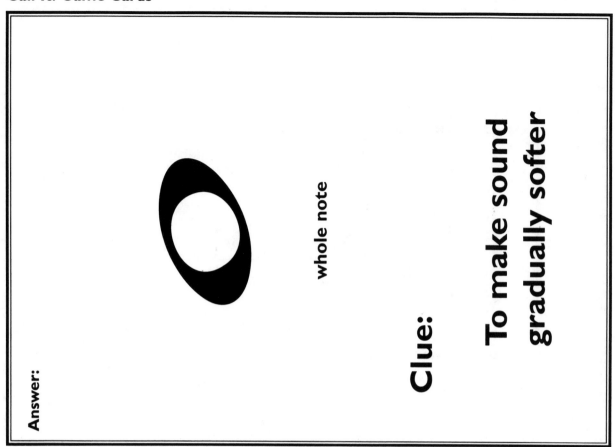

Answer:

whole note

Clue:

To make sound gradually softer

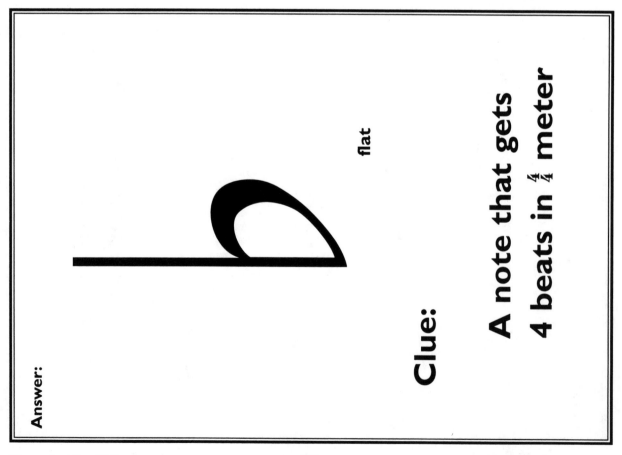

Answer:

flat

Clue:

A note that gets 4 beats in $\frac{4}{4}$ meter

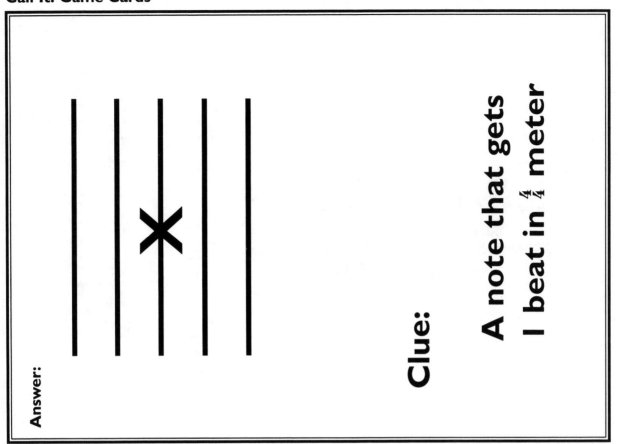

Answer:

Clue:

A note that gets 1 beat in $\frac{4}{4}$ meter

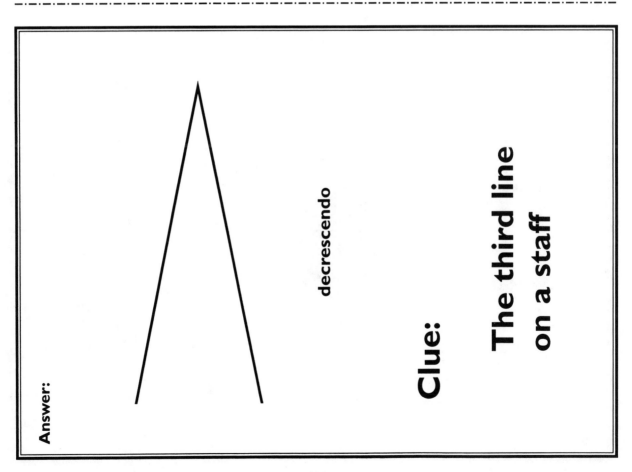

Answer:

decrescendo

Clue:

The third line on a staff

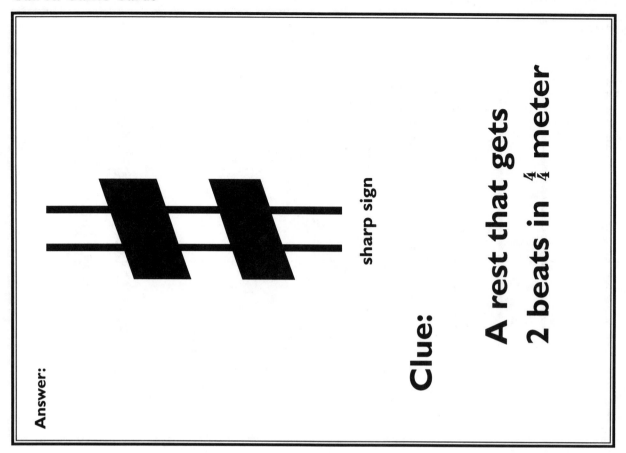

Answer:

sharp sign

Clue:

A rest that gets 2 beats in $\frac{4}{4}$ meter

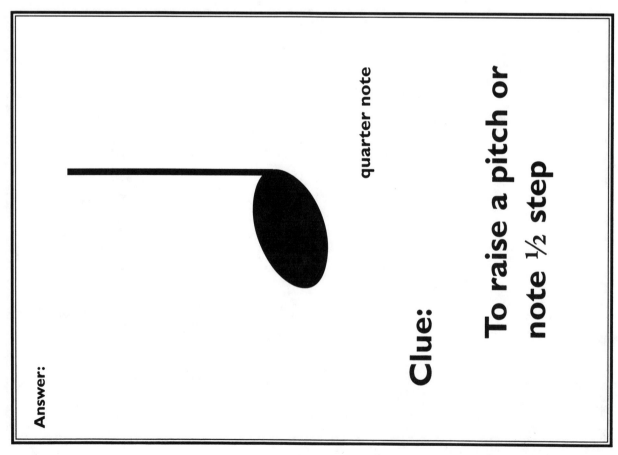

Answer:

quarter note

Clue:

To raise a pitch or note ½ step

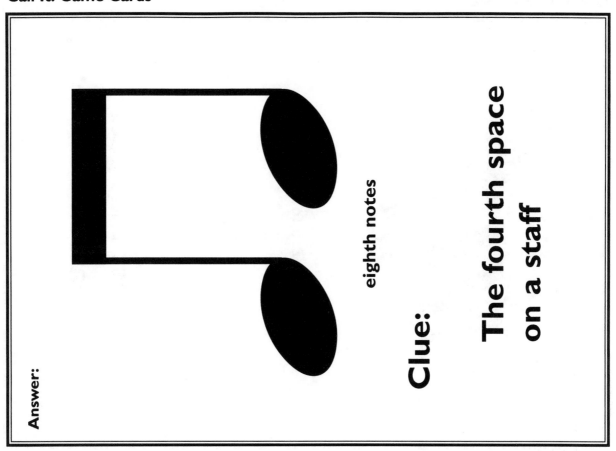

Answer:

eighth notes

Clue:

The fourth space
on a staff

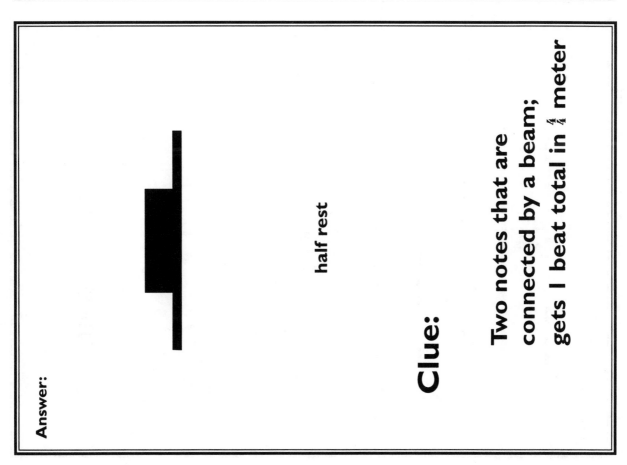

Answer:

half rest

Clue:

Two notes that are
connected by a beam;
gets 1 beat total in $\frac{4}{4}$ meter

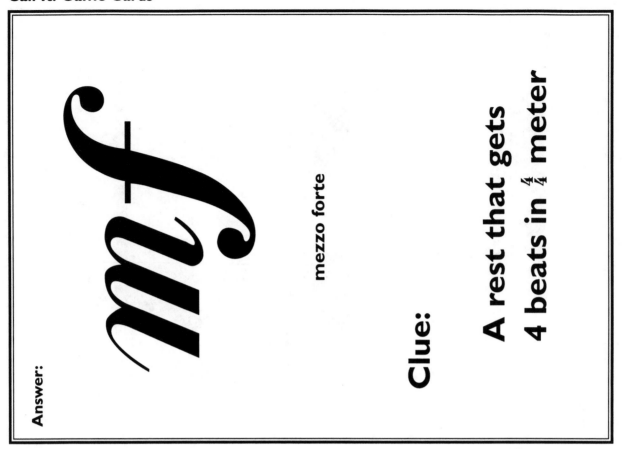

Answer:

mezzo forte

Clue:

A rest that gets 4 beats in $\frac{4}{4}$ meter

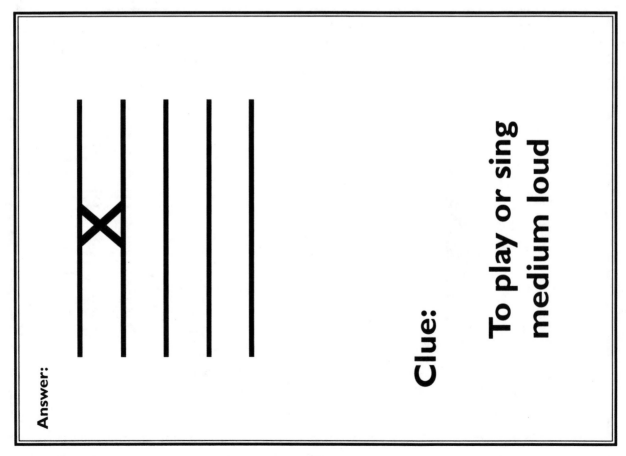

Answer:

Clue:

To play or sing medium loud

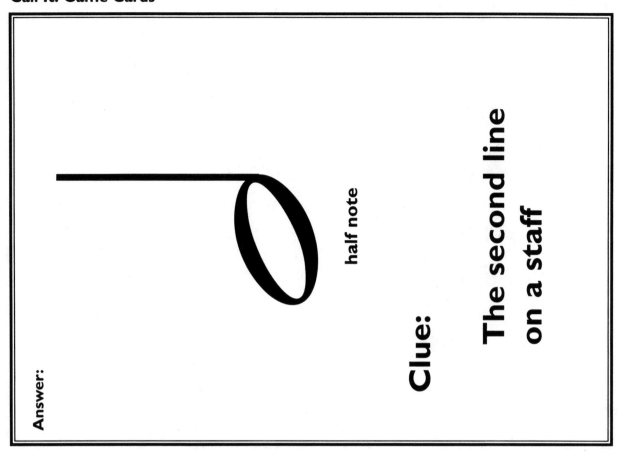

Answer:

half note

Clue:

The second line on a staff

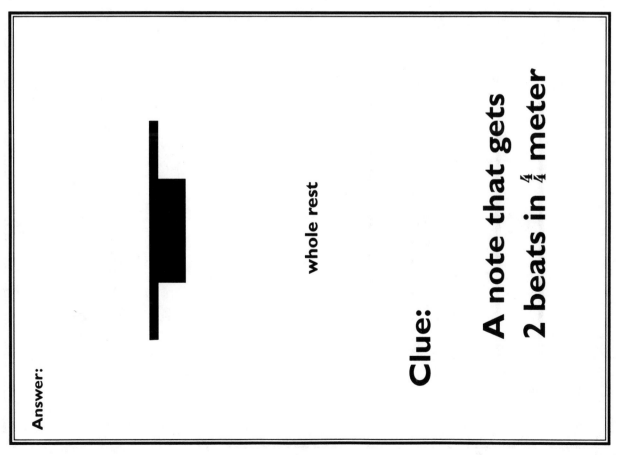

Answer:

whole rest

Clue:

A note that gets 2 beats in $\frac{4}{4}$ meter

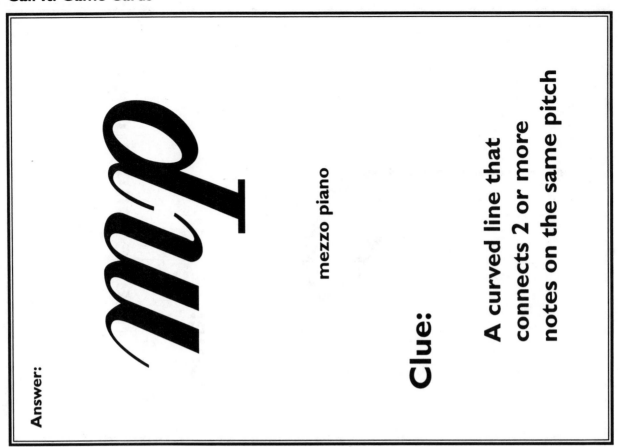

Answer:

Clue:

A curved line that connects 2 or more notes on the same pitch

mezzo piano

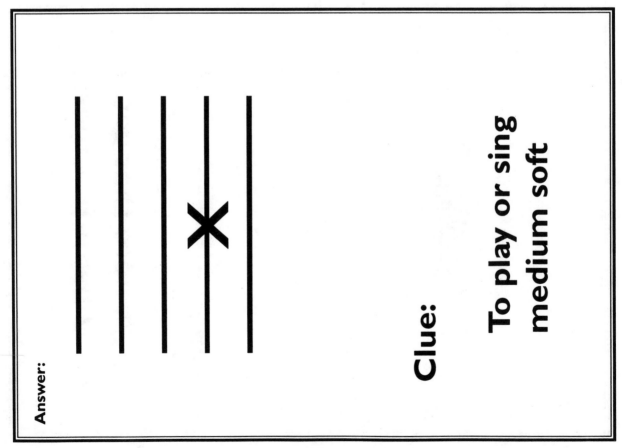

Answer:

Clue:

To play or sing medium soft

Answer:

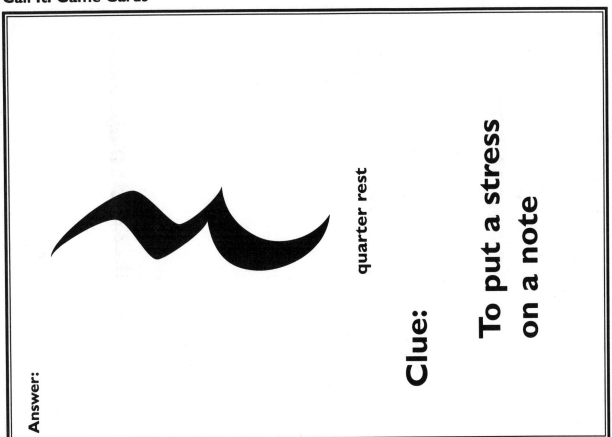

quarter rest

Clue:

To put a stress on a note

Answer:

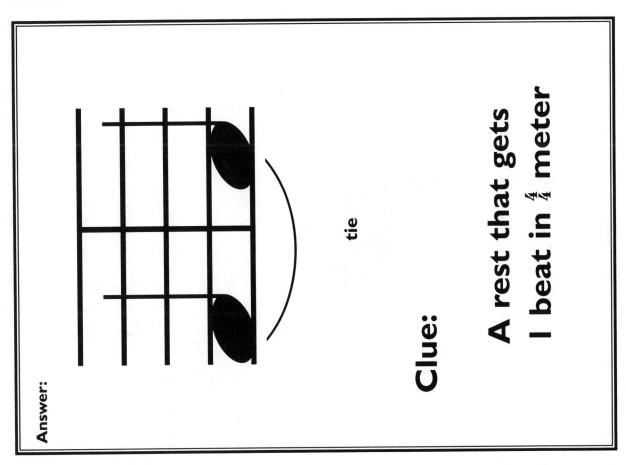

tie

Clue:

A rest that gets 1 beat in $\frac{4}{4}$ meter

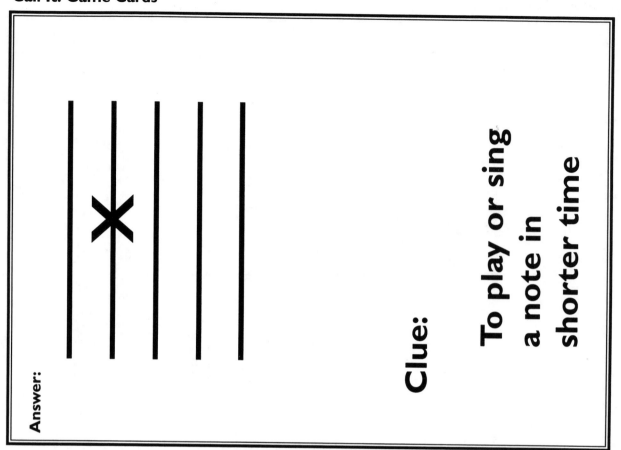

Answer:

Clue:

To play or sing a note in shorter time

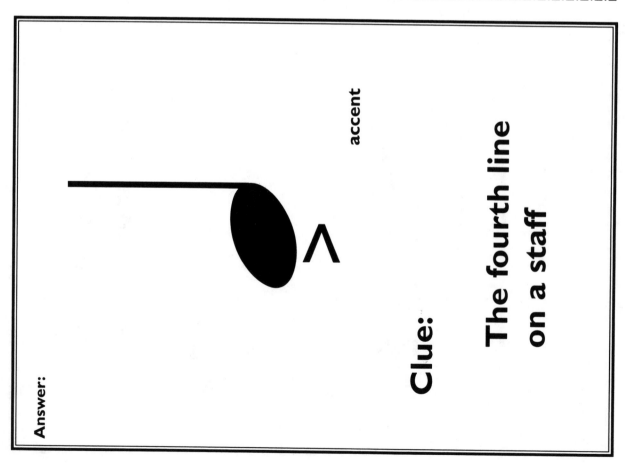

Answer:

accent

Clue:

The fourth line on a staff

Answer:

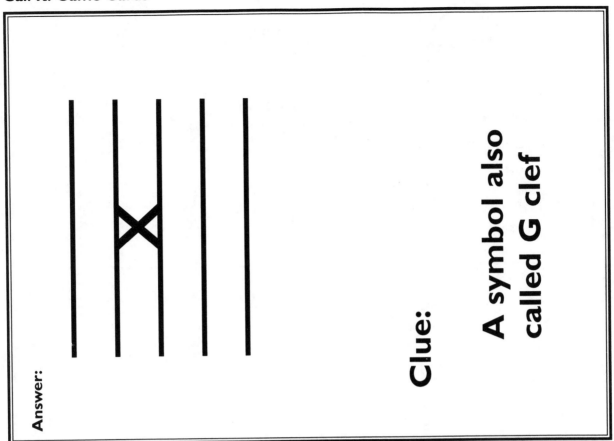

Clue:

A symbol also called G clef

Answer:

staccato

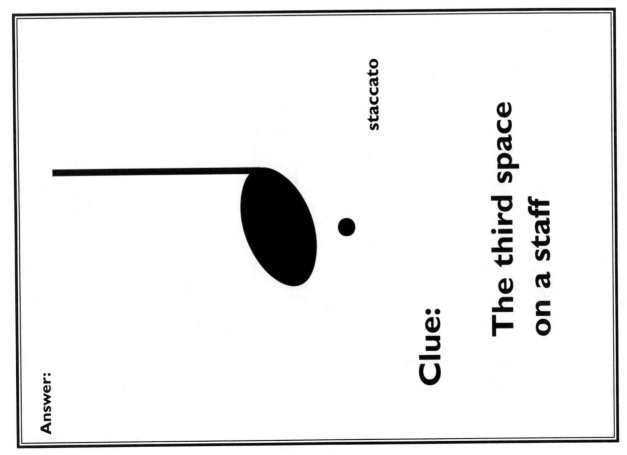

Clue:

The third space on a staff

IF20453 Big Book of Music Games

2

IF20453 *Big Book of Music Games*

5

IF20453 Big Book of Music Games

6

IF20453 Big Book of Music Games

9

IF20453 Big Book of Music Games

IF20453 *Big Book of Music Games*

IF20453 Big Book of Music Games

IF20453 Big Book of Music Games

13

IF20453 Big Book of Music Games

IF20453 Big Book of Music Games

IF20453 Big Book of Music Games

IF20453 Big Book of Music Games

 IF20453 *Big Book of Music Games*

IF20453 *Big Book of Music Games*

IF20453 *Big Book of Music Games*

22

Symbol Bingo Caller Cards

M treble clef or G clef	**U** 1st space	**S** whole note	**I** 1st line	**C** measure
M bass clef or F clef	**U** 2nd space	**S** whole rest	**I** 2nd line	**C** crescendo / decrescendo
M A, B, C, D, E, F, G — music alphabet	**U** 3rd space	**S** dotted half note	**I** 3rd line	**C** 1st & 2nd endings
M flat sign	**U** 4th space	**S** half note	**I** 4th line	**C** phrase
M sharp sign	**U** fortissimo (very loud)	**S** half rest	**I** 5th line	**C** tie

M	U	S	I	C
natural sign	mezzo forte (medium loud)	quarter note	sixteenth note	$\frac{2}{4}$ meter
staff	forte (loud)	quarter rest	sixteenth rest	$\frac{3}{4}$ meter
repeat sign	pianissimo (very soft)	dotted quarter note	triplet	$\frac{4}{4}$ meter
double bar	mezzo piano (medium soft)	eighth note	staccato	$\frac{6}{8}$ meter
bar lines	piano (soft)	eighth rest	accent	fermata

Baseball Forte Game Cards

"Single" Point to the treble clef sign. 𝄞	**"Home Run"** Point to the triplet ♫♫ 3	**"Single"** Point to the whole note. 𝅝
"Single" Point to the double bar. 𝄁	**"Home Run"** Point to the sixteenth rest. 𝄿	**"Single"** Point to the quarter note. ♩
"Triple" Point to 2 eighth notes. ♫	**"Double"** Point to the whole rest. ▬	**"Double"** Point to the fermata sign. 𝄐
"Single" Point to the four-four meter. 4/4	**"Single"** Point to 4 eighth notes. ♫♫	**"Single"** Point to 4 sixteenth notes. ♬♬

"Single"	"Home Run"	"Double"
Point to an eighth rest.	Point to the sixteenth note.	Point to the half note.
"Single"	"Single"	"Double"
Point to the quarter rest.	Point to the bass clef sign.	Point to the sharp sign.
"Double"	"Triple"	"Triple"
Point to the flat sign.	Point to the half rest.	Point to 2 sixteenth notes.
"Single"	"Double"	"Single"
Point to three-four meter.	Point to the natural sign.	Point to six-eight meter.

"Single"	"Single"	"Single"
Point to an eighth note.	Point to the dotted quarter note.	Point to the dotted half note.
♪	♩.	𝅗𝅥.
"Single"	"Single"	"Single"
Point to two-four meter.	Point to the repeat sign.	Point to the dotted quarter rest.
2/4	‖: :‖	𝄽.

Innings	Team A	Team B
1	Score:	Score:
2	Score:	Score:
3	Score:	Score:
4	Score:	Score:
5	Score:	Score:
6	Score:	Score:
7	Score:	Score:
8	Score:	Score:
9	Score:	Score:
Totals		

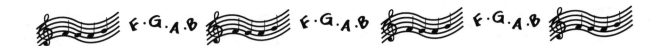

Reading Notes On a Staff

Reading Notes on a Staff

Notes on Staff Presto!

Players: Teams of 5 children
Object: To identify the notes correctly
Materials: Pattern pages 172–179, scissors, glue, different colors of construction paper, large envelopes

Preparation: Photocopy a set of pattern pages 172–178 for each team of children. (Remove the names of the notes on the first set of photocopies and then use this set when duplicating additional sets.) Mount the copies on construction paper. Cut apart the cards. To provide a set of cards for the "Caller," reproduce pattern pages 172–178, including the names of the notes. Mount these cards on a different color of construction paper. Cut apart the cards. Store the sets in large envelopes.

For an easier version of "Presto!" (identifying notes on the treble clef), duplicate pattern page 179 and cut out the Caller's cards. Use the appropriate player cards. To help the Caller, the notes on the staff shown in the first octave are indicated with the numeral "1" on page 179.

Directions: Choose one child to be the "Caller" and one child to be the "Timer." Divide the class into teams of five children. Give each team a set of cards which are distributed to all team players. To begin play, place the Caller's cards *face down* in a pile. The Caller draws three cards and announces the names of the notes. If any players have the corresponding cards, the players must hold the cards above their heads or move to a predetermined location. This must be done within 30 seconds (or an appropriate length of time). Each team which correctly identifies the notes within the time limit is awarded a game point. When all of the caller cards have been used, reshuffle and the cards and use them again. At this time, have the members of each team choose different cards to hold. Play as many rounds as appropriate for the children.

Name It! Treble Clef

Players: 2
Object: To identify/mark all notes on a game board
Materials: Pattern pages 180-181 and 188, scissors, colored file folder, construction paper, game markers, glue, watercolor markers

Preparation: Reproduce the pattern pages and color the copies if desired. Mount pages 180-181 on a file folder. To prepare the game cards, glue the copies to construction paper, then cut the cards apart.

Directions: Invite two children to play this identification game. Let each player select a panel on the game board. Place the game cards *face down* on a flat surface in a pile. To begin the game, the first player draws a card and locates the corresponding staff. If a match is made, the player marks the staff with a game marker and keeps the card. If a match cannot be made, the player loses that turn and returns the card to the bottom of the draw pile. Continue playing until one player has marked all notes on his or her game board panel. When a game is finished, have the players switch game panels and play again.

Variation: For "Name It! Bass Clef," see pattern pages 182-183 and 189. Play the game in the same manner.

Name It! Treble and Bass Clefs

Players: 4 or less
Object: To identify/mark all notes on a game board
Materials: Pattern pages 184–189, scissors, glue, game markers, construction paper

Preparation: Reproduce the patterns and mount them on construction paper. Cut apart the pieces.

Directions: See "Name It! Treble Clef."

Treble Clef Bingo

Players: 15 or more
Object: The first player to cover all notes is the winner.
Materials: Pattern pages 172–174, 178, and 190–204, scissors, construction paper, game markers, glue

Preparation: Photocopy the bingo card patterns and pattern pages 172–174 and 178. (*Note:* If you need more than 15 bingo cards, duplicate a second copy of each pattern page. Some students will use identical cards. Instead of one winner, there might be two winners for each round.) Mount the copies on construction paper. Cut apart the game cards for the "Caller." Discard the game card that shows "B" above one ledger line.

Directions: To begin play, have the Caller draw a game card and announce the name of the note. Decide how to indicate where the note is located. For example, identify the line or space on which the note is located or indicate in which octave the note is found. Each player marks the corresponding space on her or his bingo board. Continue playing in this manner until someone covers all notes on her or his bingo board.

Variation: For "Bass Clef Bingo" see pattern pages 175–178 and 205–219. Discard the game card that shows "D" below one ledger line. Play the game in the same manner.

Grand Staff Bingo

Players: 30
Object: The first player to cover all notes is the winner.
Materials: Pattern pages 172–178 and 220–250, glue, scissors, construction paper, game markers

Preparation: Follow the same procedure used for "Treble Clef Bingo" and "Bass Clef Bingo," except discard the Caller's cards that show "B" above one ledger

line and "D" below one ledger line. If additional bingo cards are needed, use pattern page 250 to create your own cards.

Directions: See "Treble Clef Bingo."

Three on Treble

Players: 2
Object: To cover 3 notes on a line or space
Materials: Pattern pages 252–255, colored file folders, construction paper, watercolor markers, scissors, glue

Preparation: Reproduce the pattern pages and color them as desired. Mount pages 252-253 on a file folder. Carefully match the lines on the staff to complete the picture. Mount pages 254-255 in the same manner. Prepare three copies of page 251 and mount them on construction paper, then cut out the game pieces.

Directions: Have the players sit with the game boards in front of them. Place the game pieces *face down* and mix them up. The first player draws a game piece and matches it on the game board. If that note is not shown on the staff, the game piece is returned to the draw pile. If the note is shown on the staff, the game piece is placed on the corresponding note. Continue playing until one player has marked three notes on a line or space. When the game is finished, have the players exchange game boards and play again.

Variations: For "Three on Bass," see pattern pages 256–259. Follow the same procedure to play this game.

When the students can easily read notes on the treble staff and the bass staff, let a group of four or fewer children play "Three on Treble or Bass." Use the materials for "Three on Treble" and Three on Bass." Give each player a game board. Play the game in the same manner as "Three on Treble." Be sure to notice how middle C is indicated with a line drawn through the "C." The player must identify the position of the note (above or below middle "C").

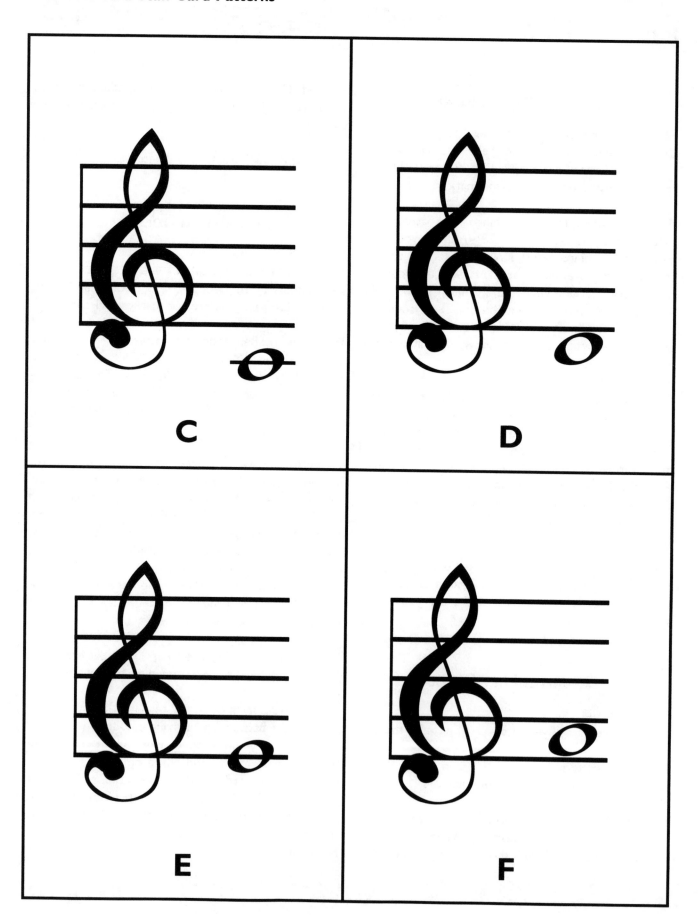

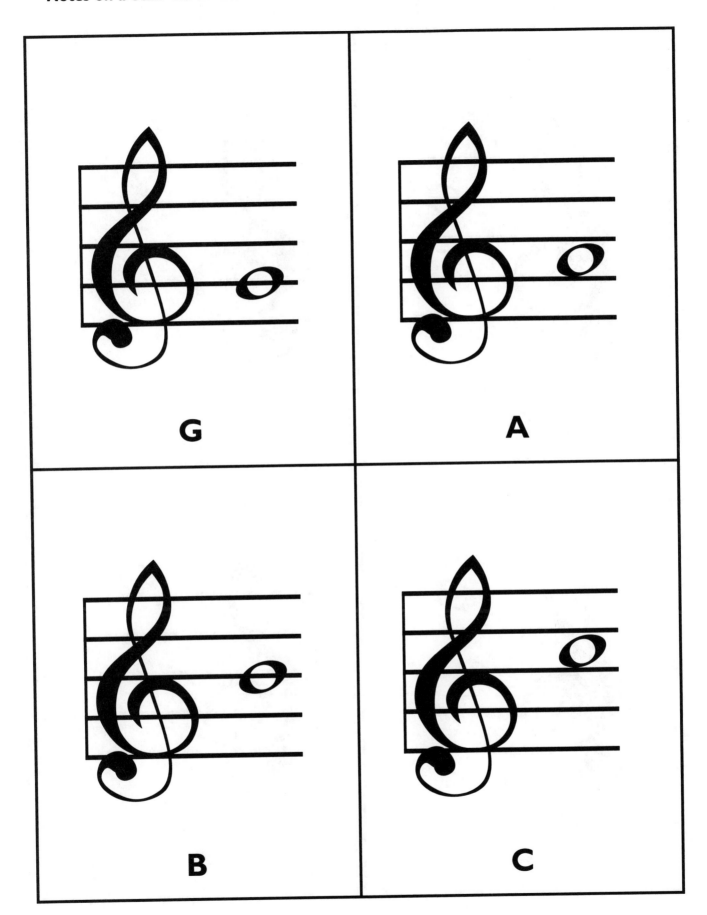

G

A

B

C

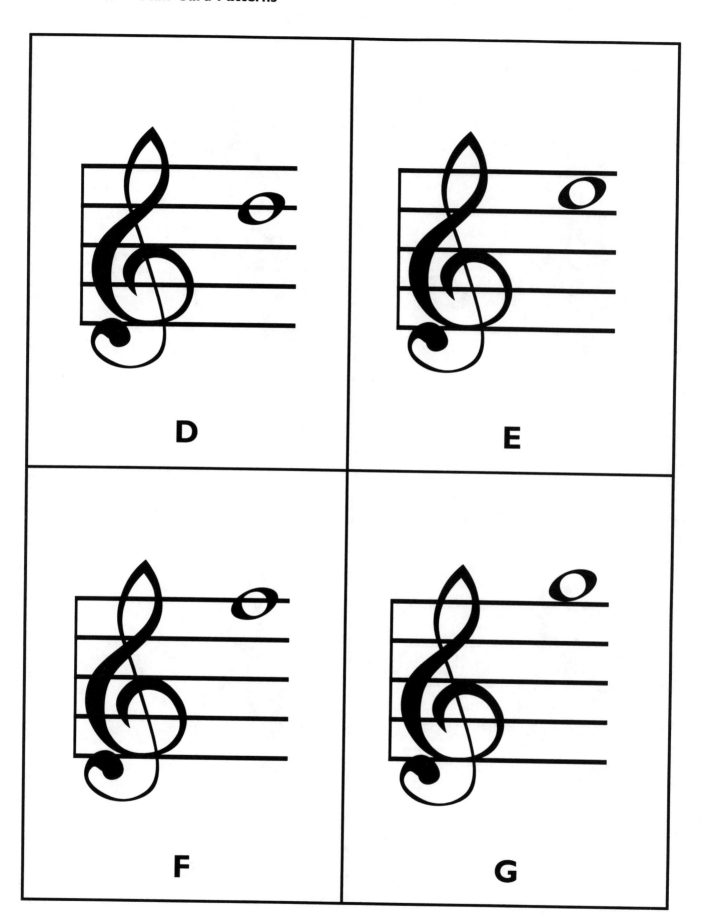

Notes on a Staff Card Patterns

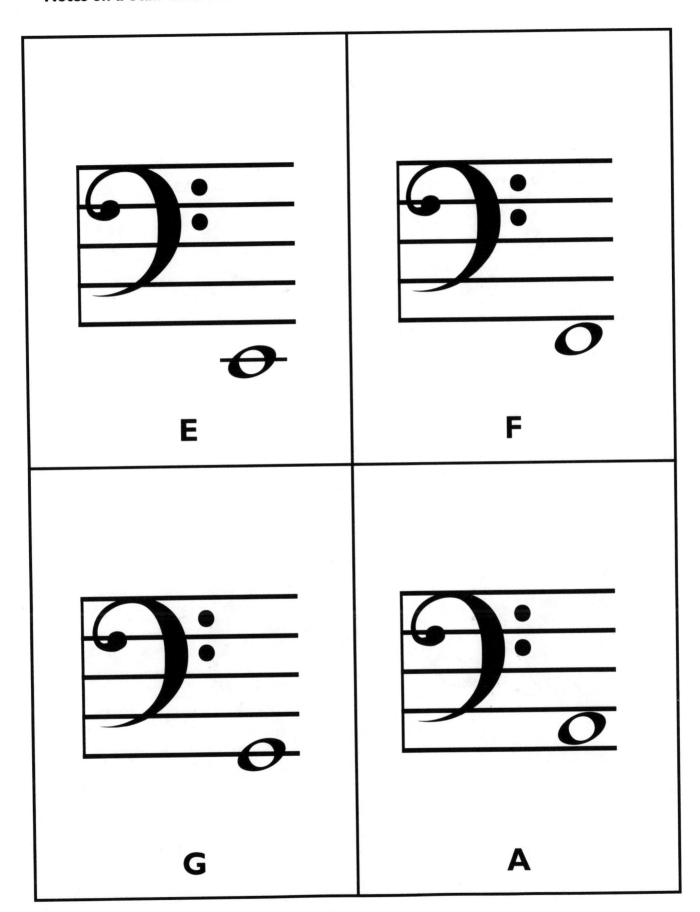

E

F

G

A

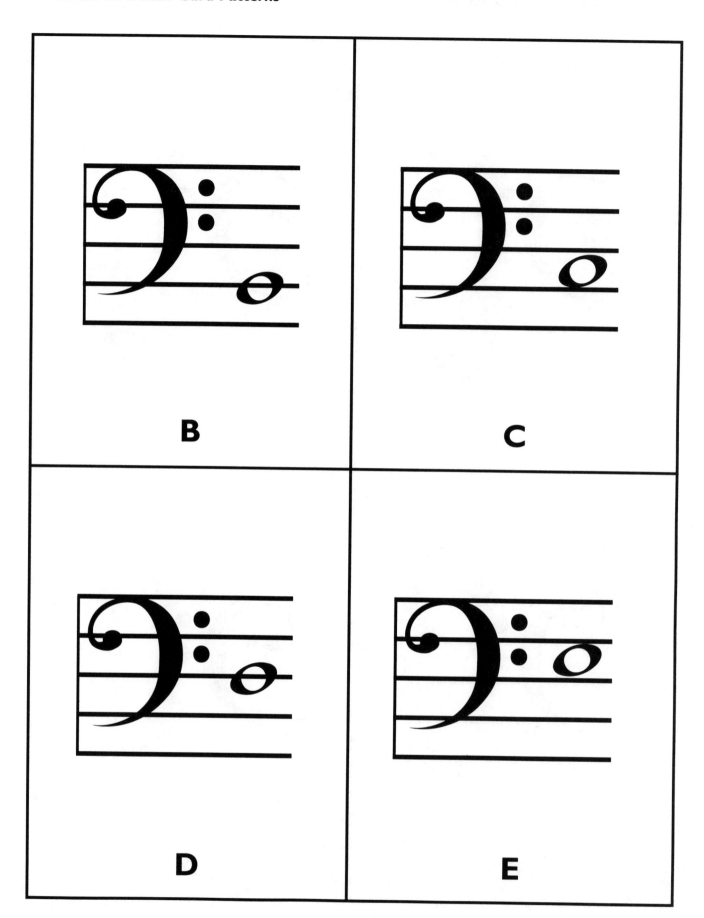

B

C

D

E

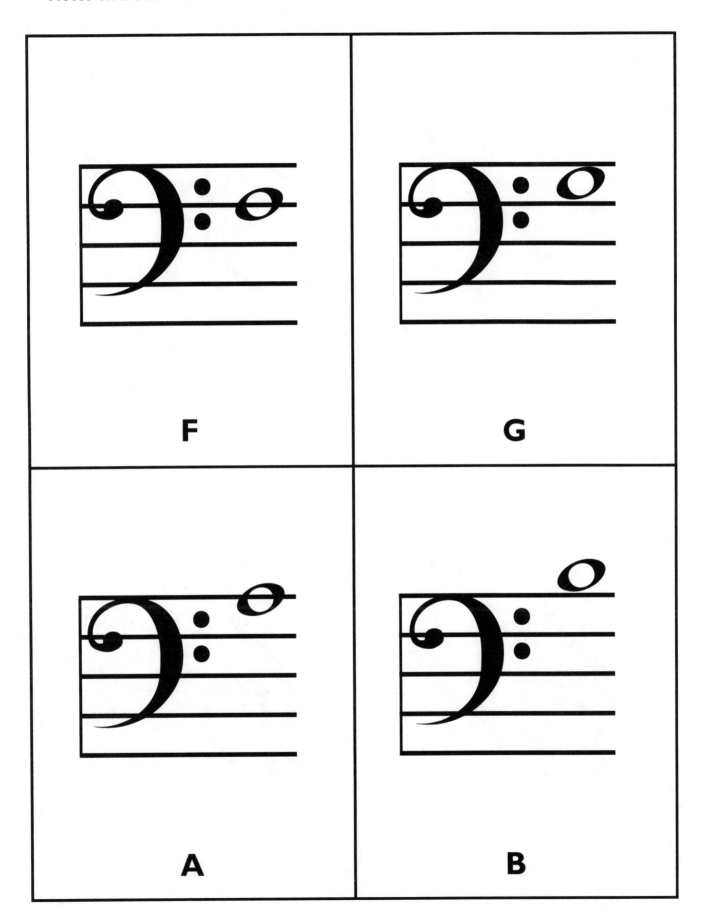

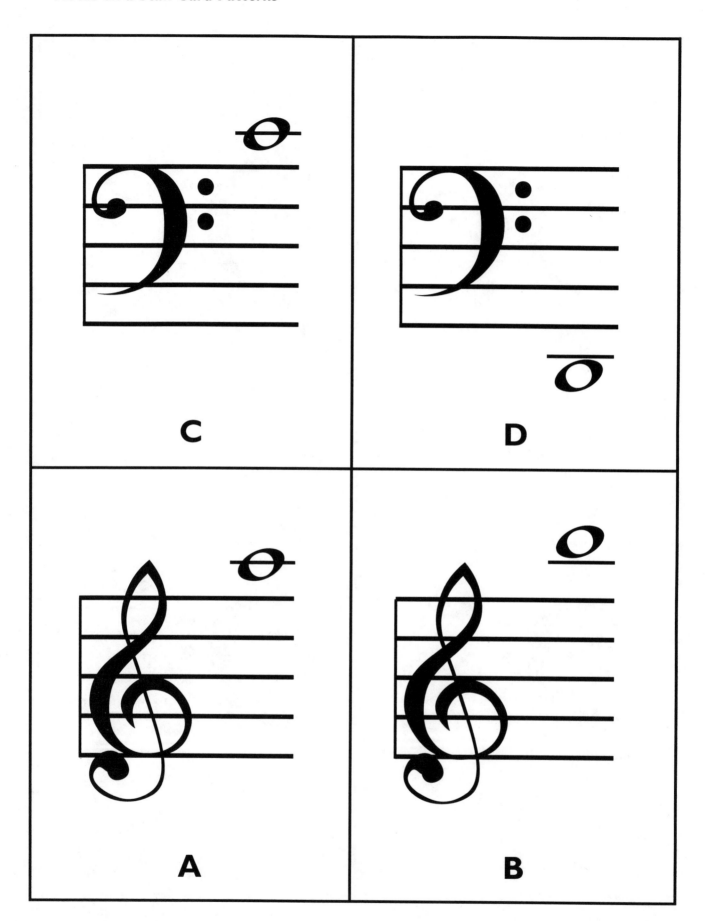

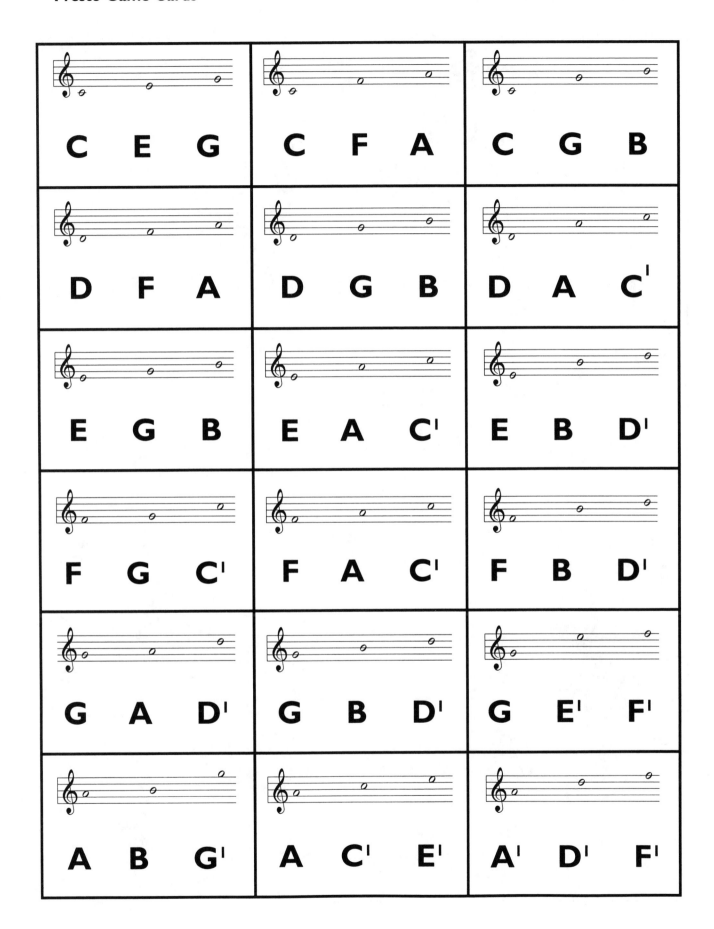

B

𝄞 C	𝄞 D	𝄞 E
𝄞 F	𝄞 G	𝄞 A
𝄞 B	𝄞 C	𝄞 D
𝄞 E	𝄞 F	𝄞 G
𝄞 A	𝄞 B	Take a rest!

𝄢 C	𝄢 D	𝄢 E
𝄢 F	𝄢 G	𝄢 A
𝄢 B	𝄢 C	𝄢 B
𝄢 A	𝄢 G	𝄢 F
𝄢 E	𝄢 D	**Take a rest!**

Treble Clef Bingo

2

5

14

15

IF20453 Big Book of Music Games

4

7

Bass Clef Bingo

Bass Clef Bingo

12

216

13

Grand Staff Bingo

♪A♪B♪C♪D♪E♪F♪G♪A♪B♪C♪D♪E♪F♪G♪

1

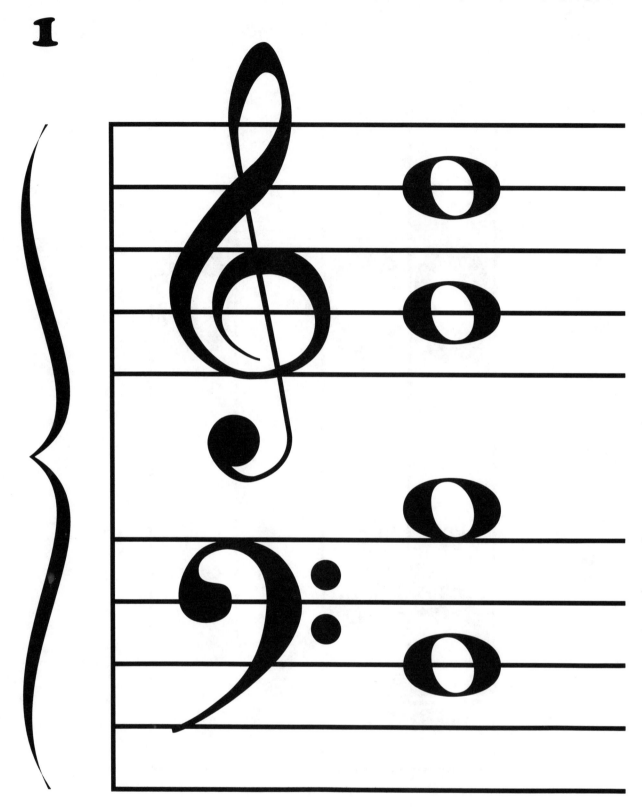

♪A♪B♪C♪D♪E♪F♪G♪A♪B♪C♪D♪E♪F♪G♪

2

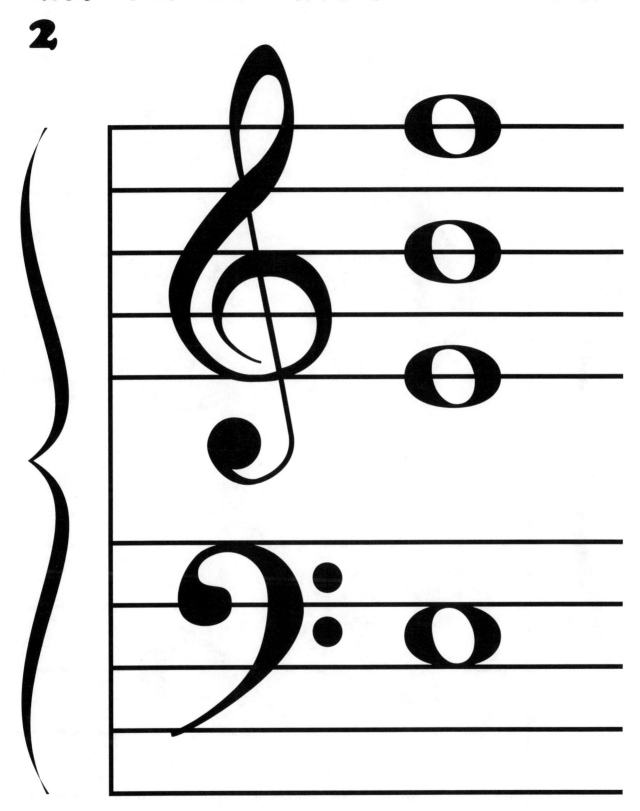

IF20453 *Big Book of Music Games*

3

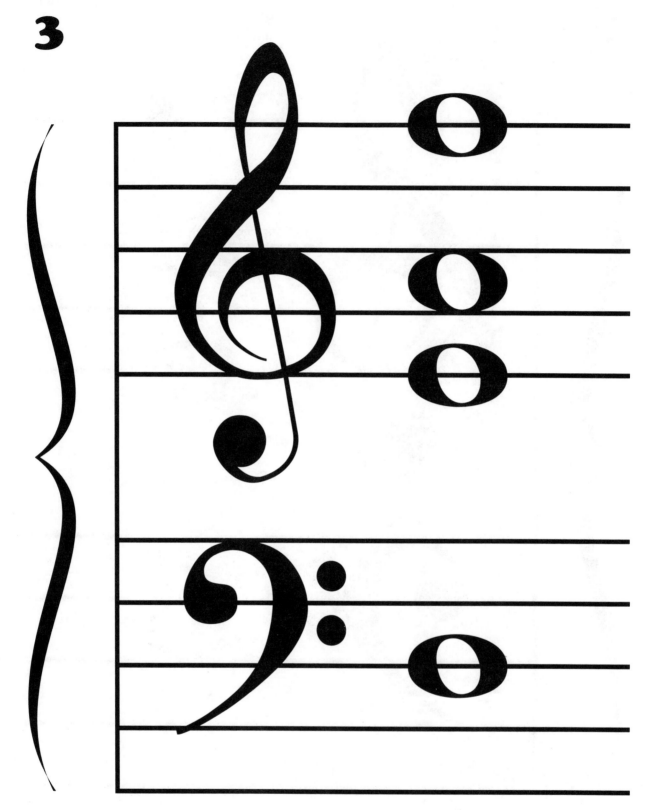

4

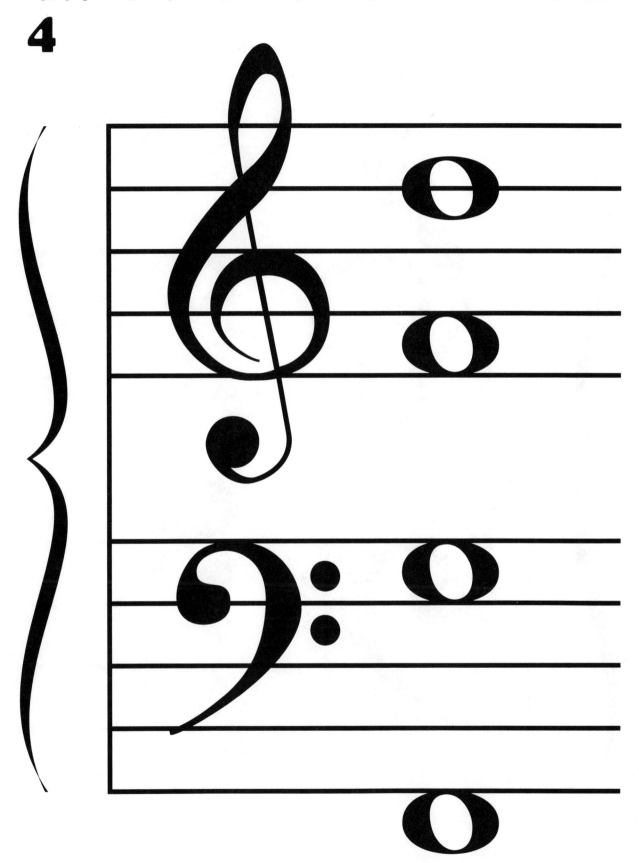

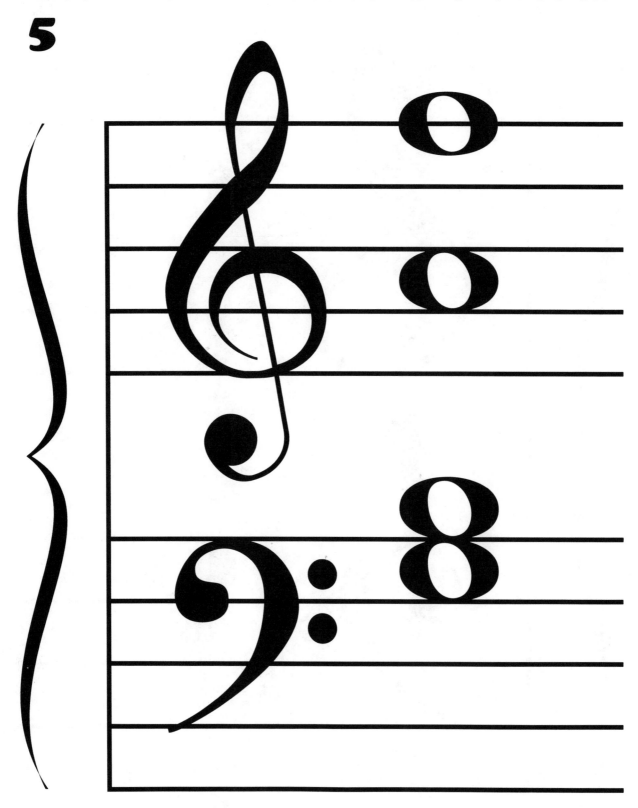

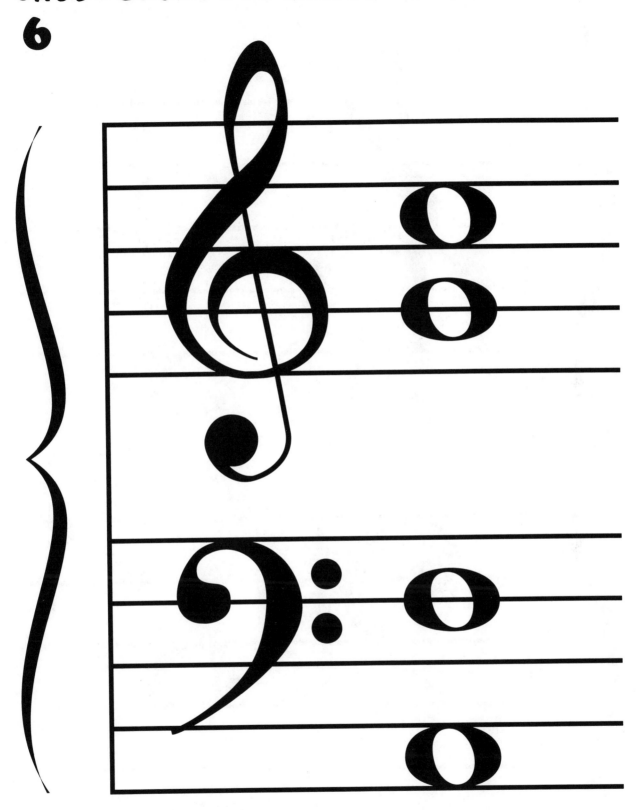

8

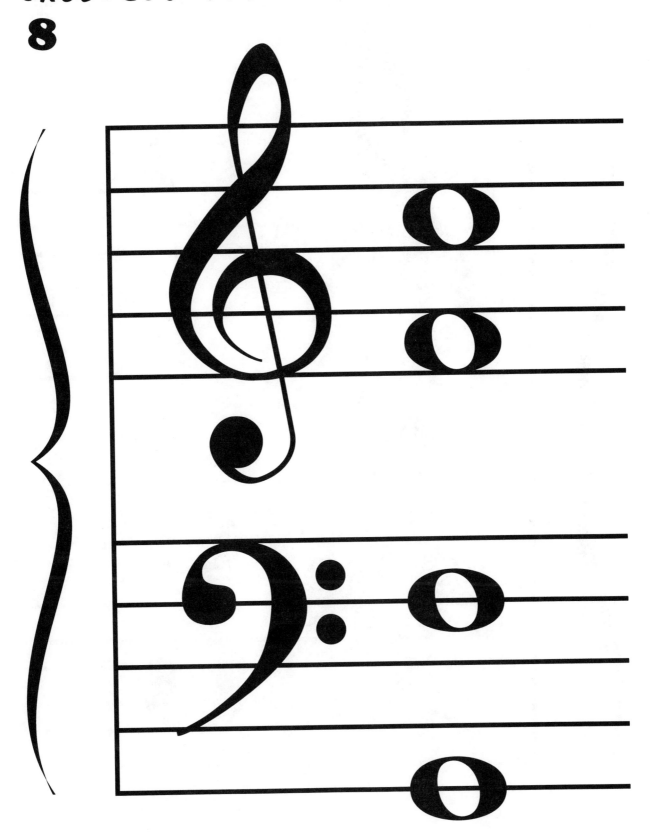

9

10

IF20453 *Big Book of Music Games*

12

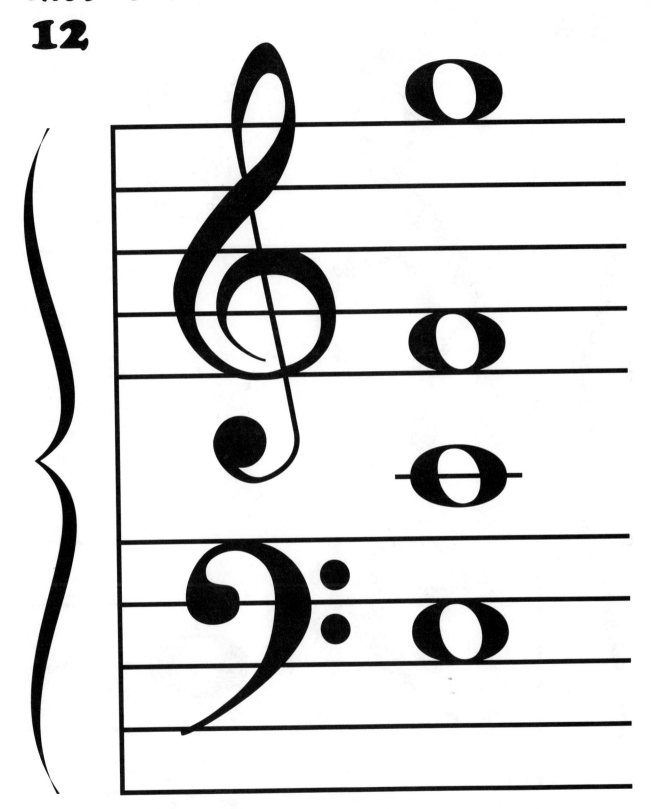

231

13

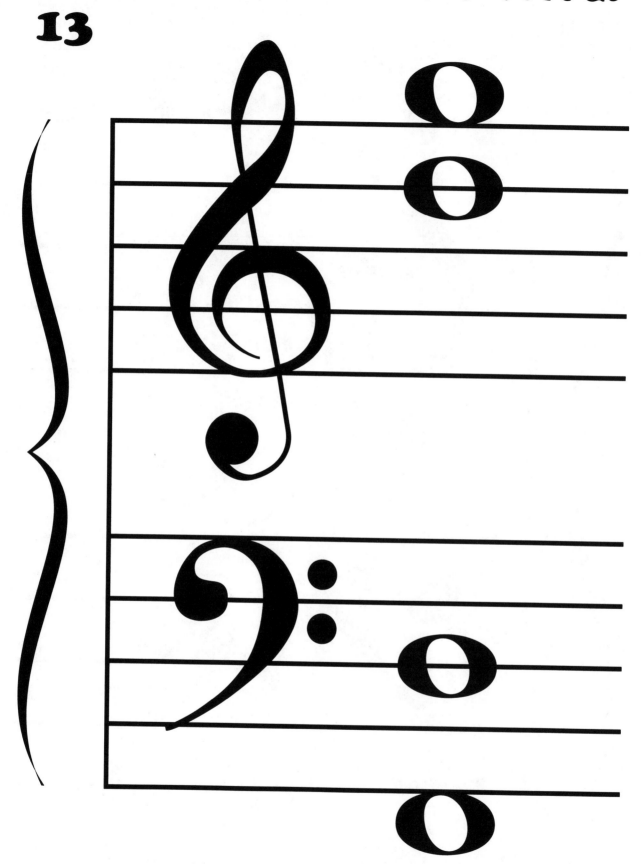

232

14

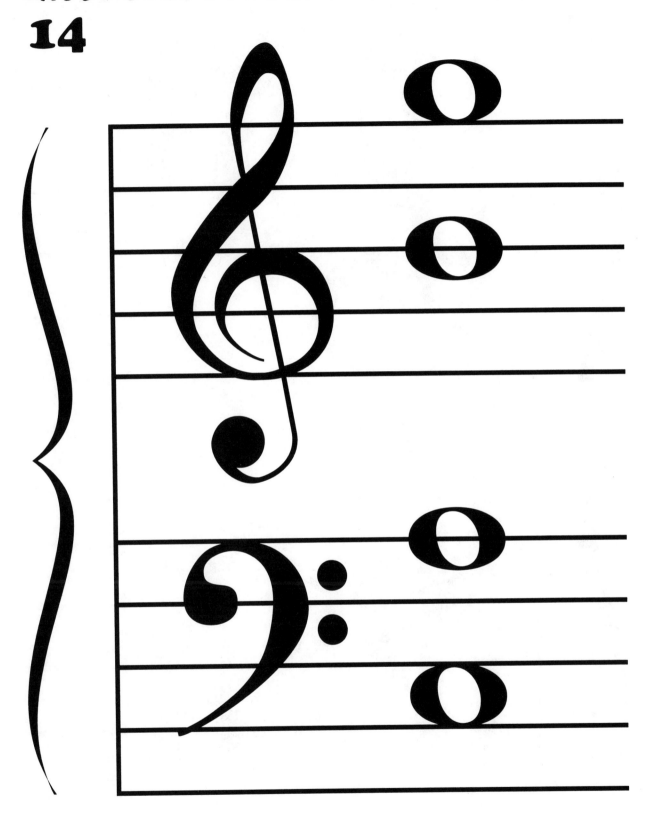

IF20453 Big Book of Music Games

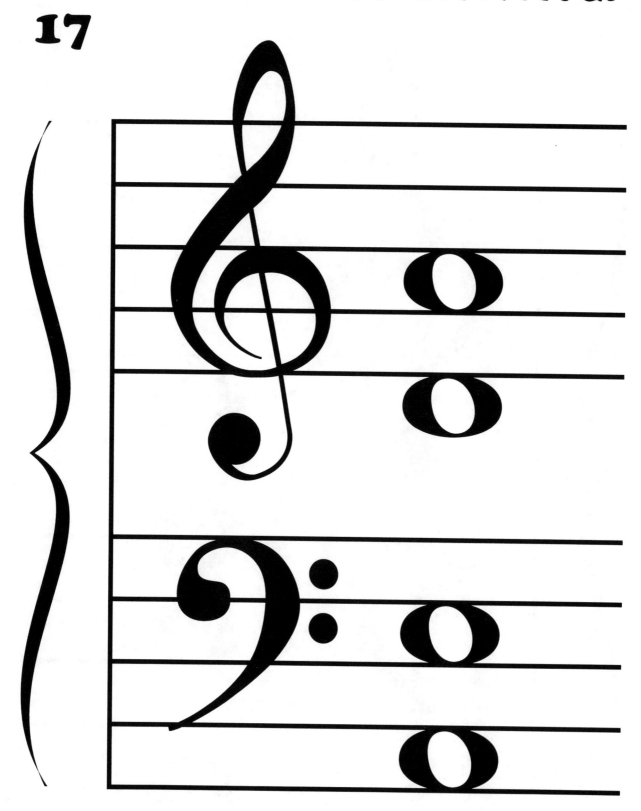

236

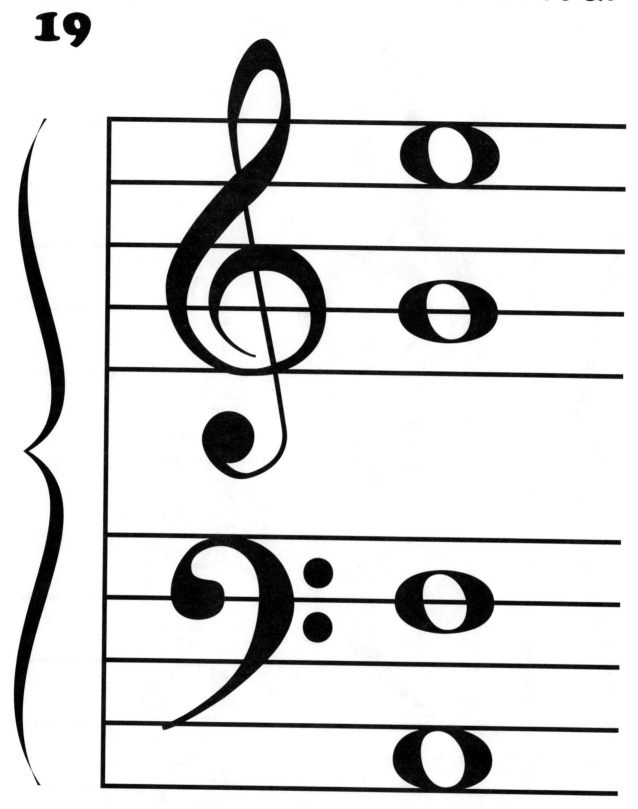

21

22

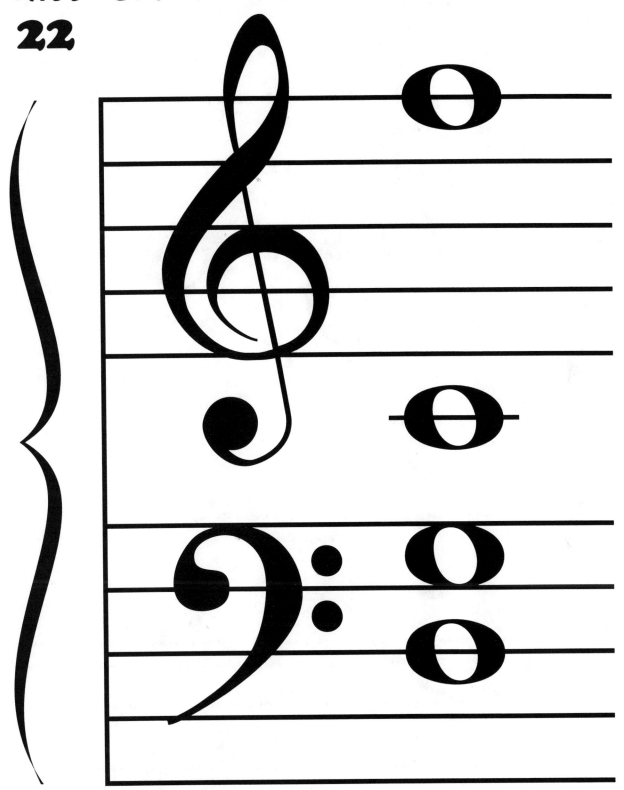

241

23

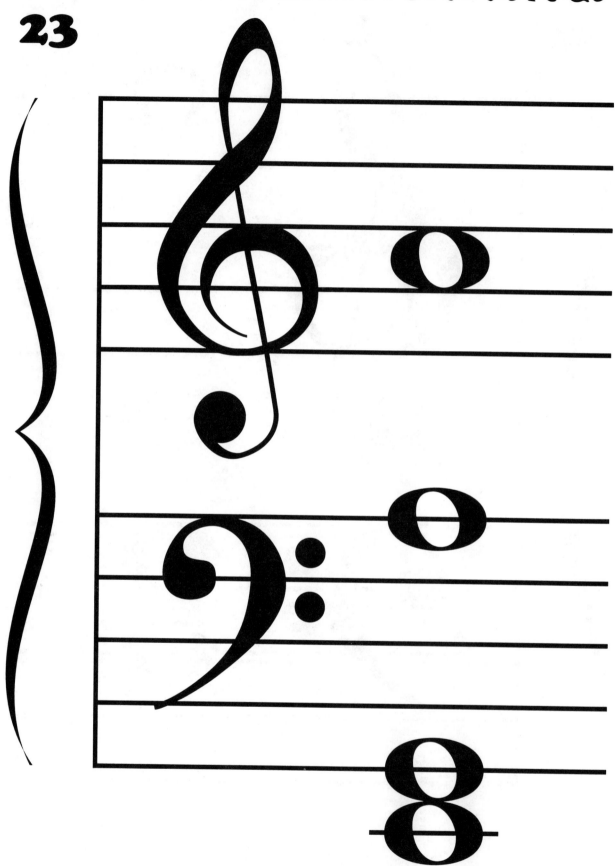

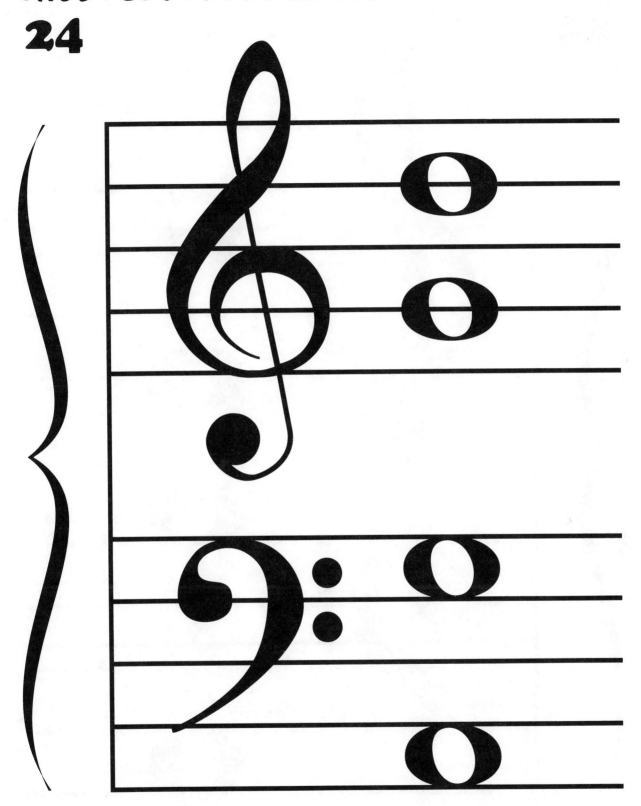

 IF20453 *Big Book of Music Games*

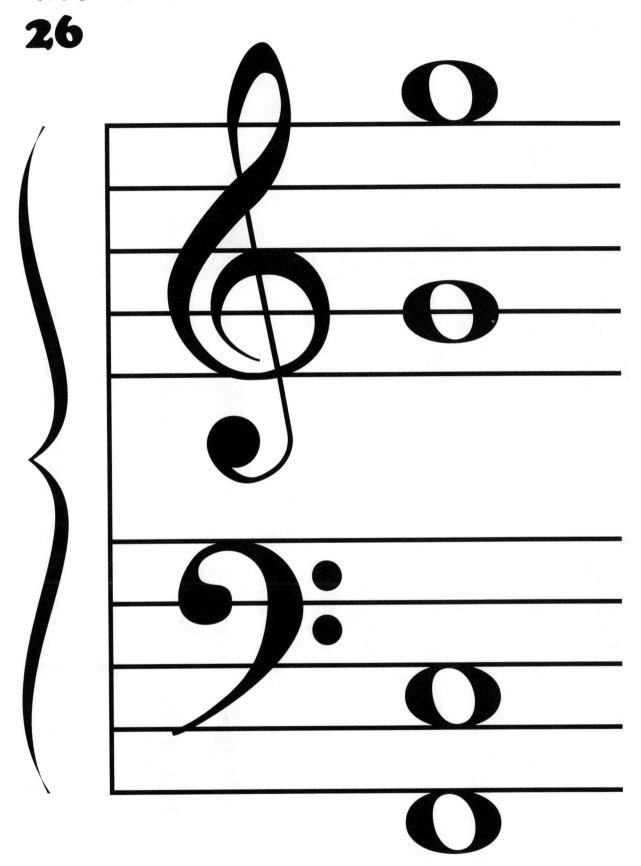

27

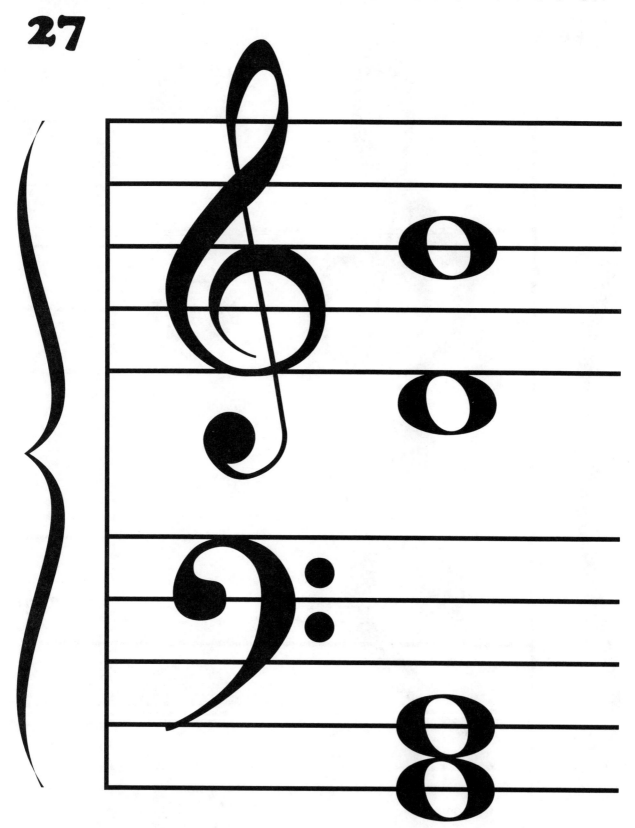

246   IF20453 *Big Book of Music Games*

28

29

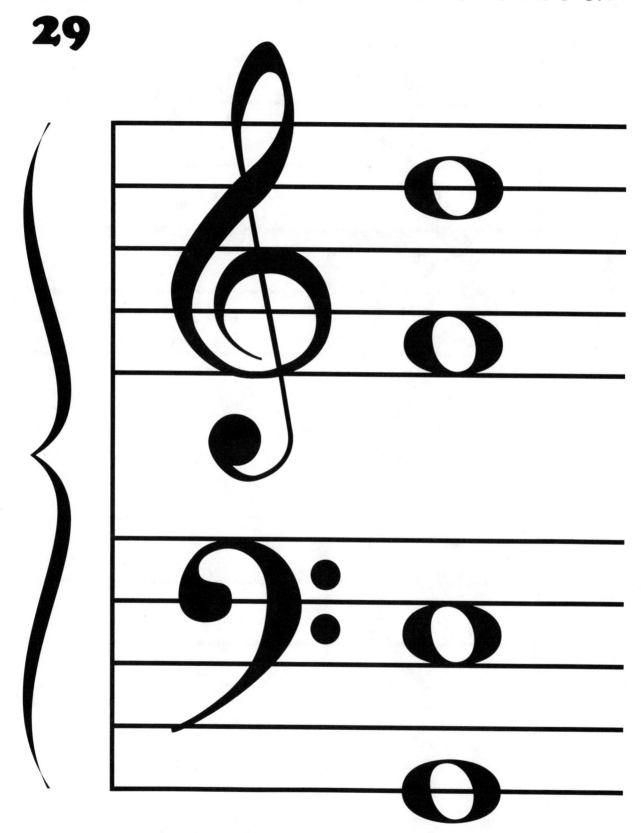

© Instructional Fair • TS Denison · 248 · IF20453 *Big Book of Music Games*

30

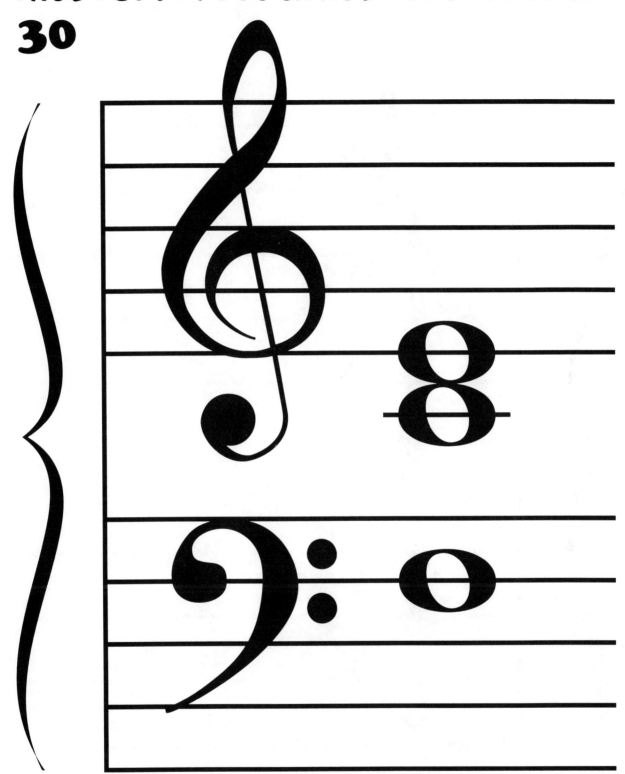

IF20453 Big Book of Music Games

Grand Staff Bingo-Blank Card

Three on Treble Game Cards

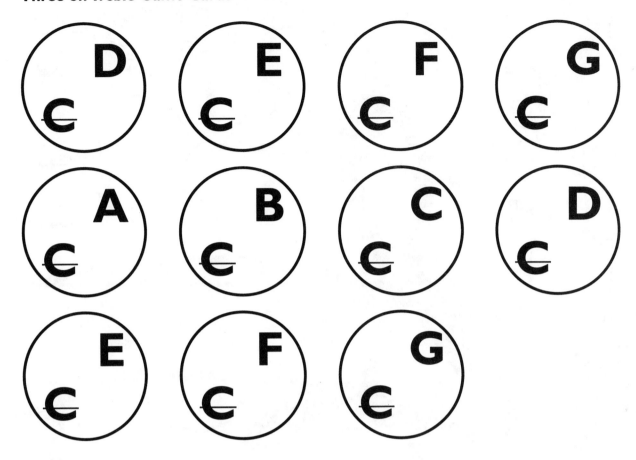

Three on Bass Game Cards

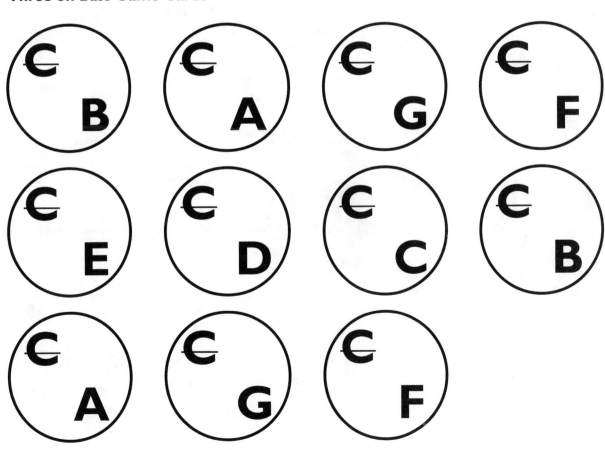

Three on Treble (Lines)

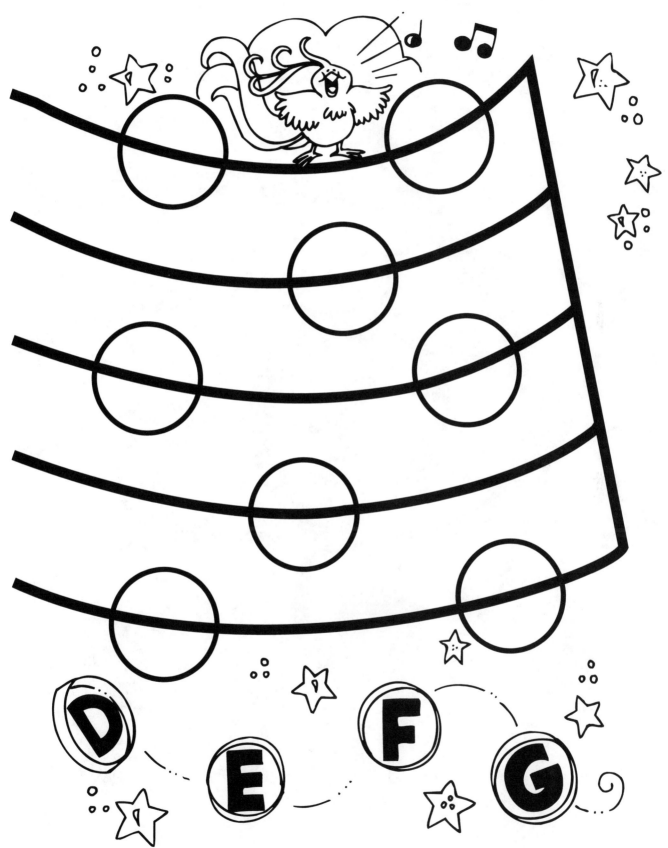

Three on Treble (Spaces)

Three on Bass (Lines)

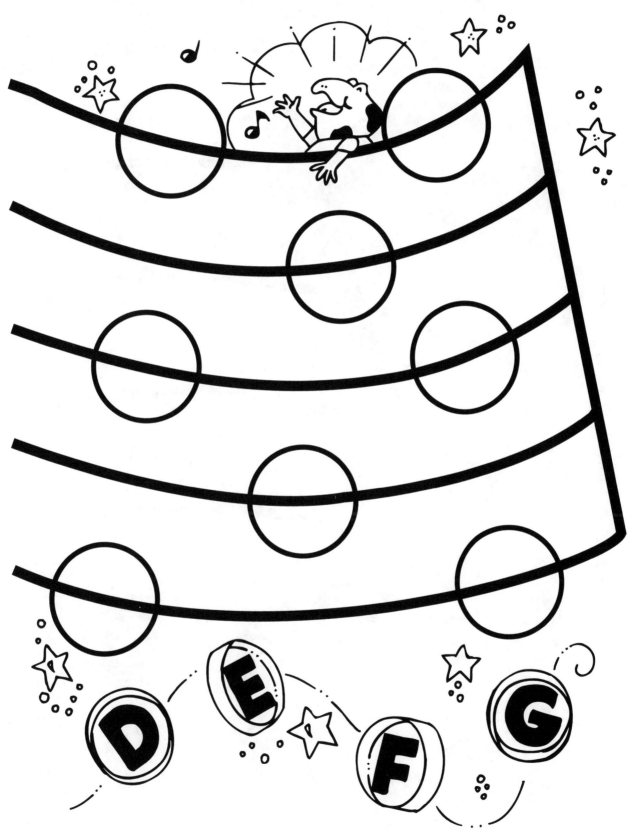

Three on Bass (Spaces)

first line	second line	third line
fourth line	fifth line	first space
second space	third space	fourth space
Take a rest!	Any Space!	Any Line!

260

Reading Intervals

Reading Intervals

Interval Presto!

Players: Teams of 5 children
Object: To identify the intervals correctly
Materials: Pattern pages 264–266, scissors, glue, different colors of construction paper, large envelopes

Preparation: Photocopy a set of pattern pages 264–266 for each team of children. (Remove the names of the intervals on the first set of photocopies and then use this set when duplicating additional sets.) Be sure to enlarge the copies before making reproductions. If appropriate, create additional interval cards with the blank card patterns. Mount the copies on construction paper. Cut apart the cards. To provide a set of cards for the "Caller," print on small pieces of construction paper the following words: repeat (twice), step up, step down, skip up, skip down, leap up, leap down, jump up, and jump down. If you prefer to use the actual interval names (unison, second, third, fourth, and fifth), print those names instead of the common terms. Store the sets in large envelopes.

Directions: Divide the class into teams of five children. Give each team a set of cards which are distributed to all team players. To begin play, place the game cards *face down* in a pile. Ask one student to be the "Caller" and one student to be the "Timer." The Caller draws a card and announces the name of the interval. If the players have the corresponding cards, they must hold the cards above their heads or move to a predetermined location. This must be done within 10 seconds (or an appropriate length of time). Each team which correctly identifies the interval within the time limit is awarded a game point. Play as many rounds as appropriate for the children.

Allegro with Intervals

Players: 2 or 3
Object: To identify the intervals correctly to reach BRAVO!
Materials: Pattern pages 264–267, scissors, construction paper, glue, watercolor markers, game marker for each player, envelope

Preparation: Duplicate the game board and mount it on construction paper. Color the game board as desired. Using the blank staff pattern, create 10 or more additional game cards for identifying intervals. Cut apart the game cards, removing the name from the bottom of each card. To make this game self-checking, provide the name of the interval on the back of each card. Be sure to include a number from 1 to 3 on the back of the card. This will indicate how many spaces the player can move if the interval is identified correctly. When finished, store the cards in an envelope.

Directions: Mix up the game cards and place them *face up* in a pile. Have each student select a game marker and place it on START. The first player draws a game card and identifies the interval. If the answer is correct, the player moves his or her game marker the corresponding number of spaces on the path. The second player takes a turn and plays in the same manner. When all game cards have been used, reshuffle and use again. Continue playing until one player reaches BRAVO!

Step, Skip, Jump Fun

Players: 5 or less
Object: To cover 3 spaces in a row or all spaces on the game board
Materials: Pattern pages 268–275, scissors, construction paper, glue, colored copier paper, marker, game markers

Preparation: Duplicate the pattern pages on white or colored paper and mount them on construction paper. To make the game self-checking, cut apart the cards and label the intervals on the backs.

Directions: Give each player a game board. Invite the players to sit in a circle with the game cards placed in the center. Have the game cards *face up* in a pile to hide the answers on the back. Decide which player starts the game. The first player draws a card and identifies the interval shown on the card. If the answer is indicated on his or her game board, the corresponding space is marked and the player keeps the game card. If the answer is not shown on the board, the game card is returned to the bottom of the draw pile. The next player takes a turn and plays in the same manner. Continue playing the game in the same manner until one player has marked three spaces in a horizontal, vertical, or diagonal row or covered all spaces. When finished, have the players exchange game boards and play again.

Variation: If you prefer to have the students identify the actual names of the intervals on their game boards, remove the common terms and replace them with the following terms: repeat, step (2nd or second), skip (3rd or third), leap (4th or fourth), jump (5th or fifth).

Reading Simple Tunes

Players: 2 or more
Object: To correctly identify intervals in music and reach AWESOME on the game board
Materials: Pattern pages 276–278, colored file folder, laminating material, scissors, glue, colored file folder, white or colored copier paper, construction paper, watercolor marker

Preparation: Reproduce all pattern pages on white or colored copier paper. Mount pages 276 and 277 on the file folder, then laminate it. Mount the game cards on construction paper and cut them apart.

Directions: To play a round, each student draws a card and identifies the interval in the music by circling the notes. If the answer is correct, the student moves his or her game marker the following number of spaces on the path: repeat (unison)–1 space, step (second)–2 spaces, skip (third)–3 spaces, leap (fourth)–4 spaces, and jump (fifth)–5 spaces. If the player is unable to locate an example of the interval, the player loses that turn. Continue playing until one player reaches AWESOME.

Variation: Perhaps the students are ready to use the actual names of the intervals. Provide game cards with those names instead of the common terms.

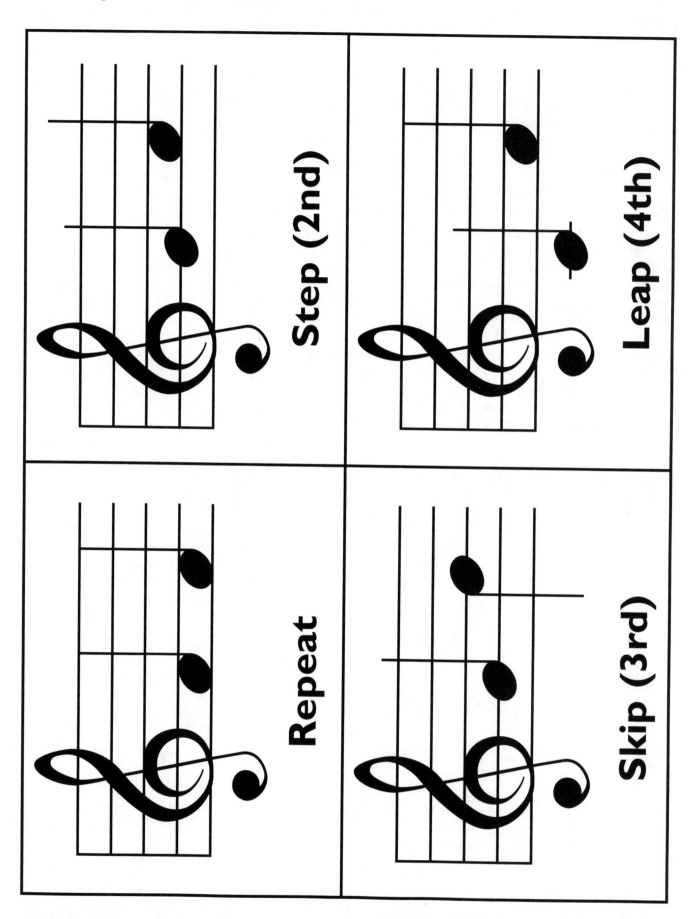

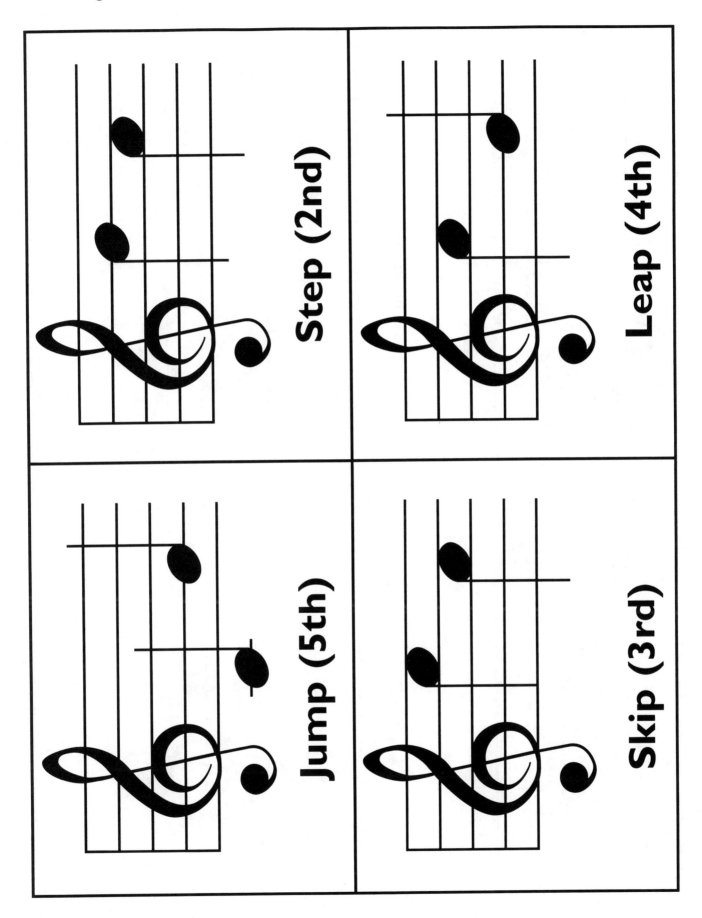

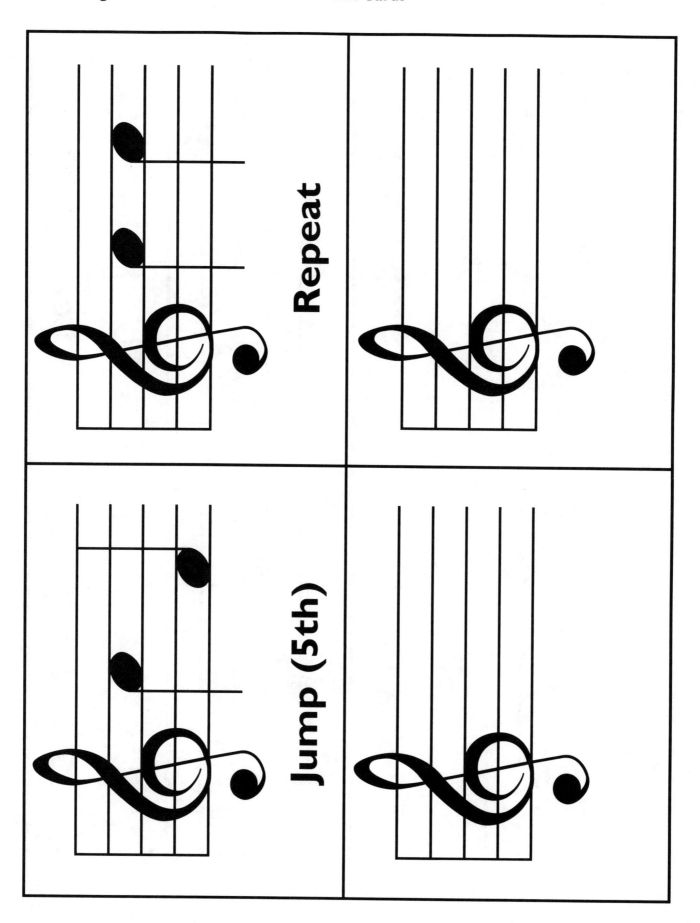

Start

Allegro with Intervals

Bravo!

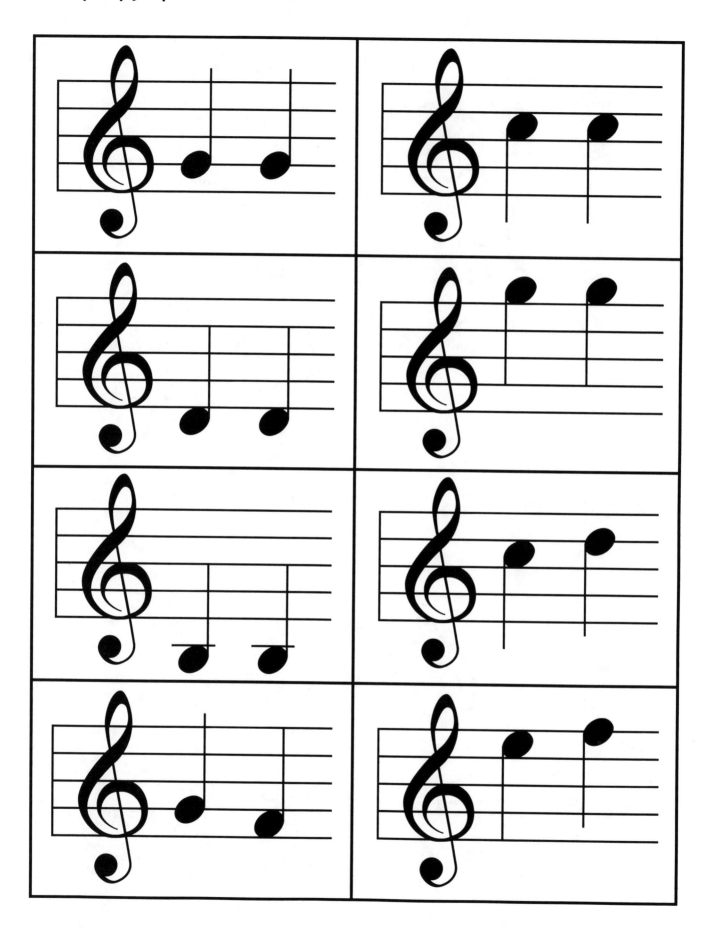

Step-Skip-Jump Fun Game Cards

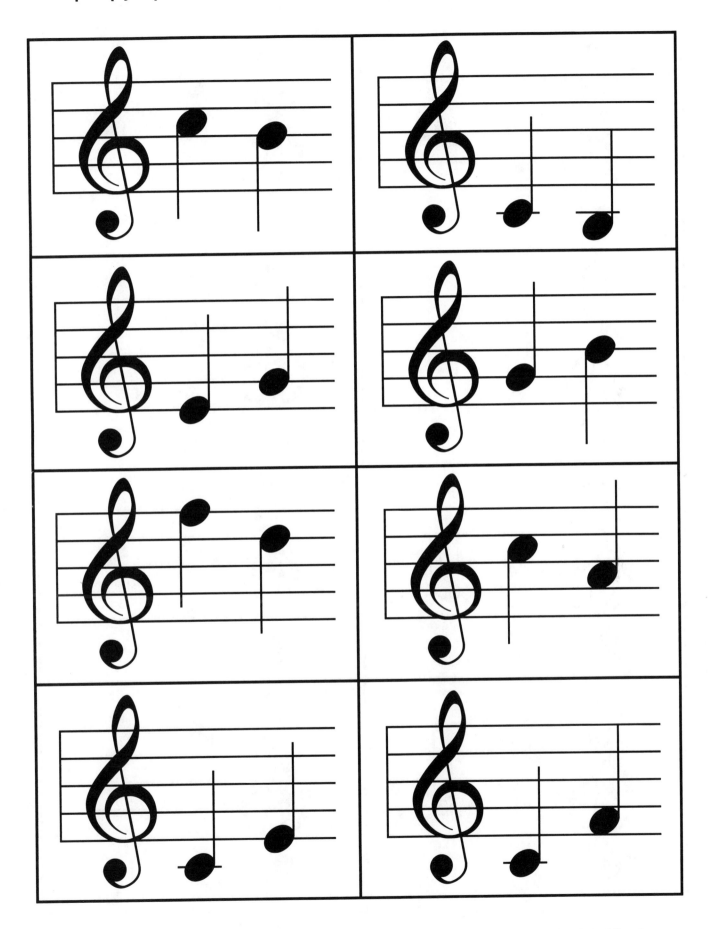

269

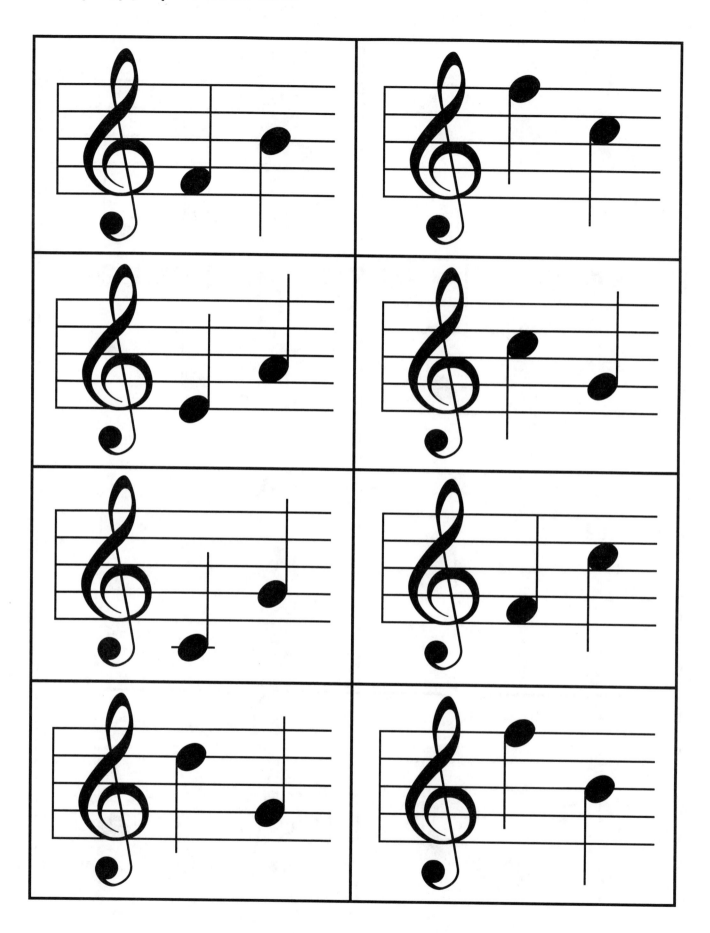

270

Step-Skip-Jump Fun

step

jump

repeat

jump

skip

leap

leap

repeat

leap

271

IF20453 *Big Book of Music Games*

Step-Skip-Jump Fun

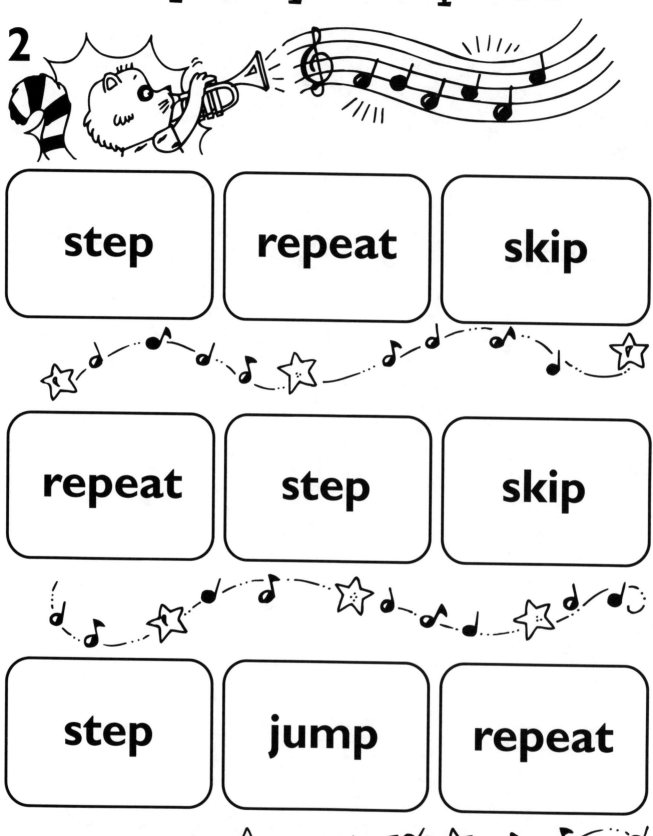

Step-Skip-Jump Fun

leap | step | leap

step | repeat | step

jump | leap | skip

Step-Skip-Jump Fun

Step-Skip-Jump Fun

5

repeat	skip	leap
skip	jump	repeat
repeat	step	step

A Tisket, A Tasket

Frère Jacques

Reading Simple Tunes

Start

Awesome!

repeat	repeat	repeat	repeat
repeat	step	step	step
step	step	skip	skip
skip	skip	leap	leap
leap	leap	jump	jump

Musical Instruments

Musical Instruments

Instrument Quest!

Players: 2
Object: The first player to reach the top of the chart is the winner.
Materials: Pattern pages 282–292, construction paper, scissors, glue, black marker, game markers

Preparation: Photocopy the pattern pages and mount them on construction paper. Cut apart the game cards on pages 282–287 and 289–292. To make the game cards self-checking, mount the clue card for an instrument on the back of the corresponding picture card. Be sure to remove the answer on the clue card before adhering it. Continue in the same manner until all clue cards have been glued to picture cards.

Directions: Have two students place the game board and clue cards within reach. Arrange the clue cards in a pile so the pictures are *face down*. Decide which player will start the round. The first player draws a clue card and identifies the instrument. If the answer is correct, the player moves his or her game marker one space ahead. If the answer is incorrect, the player loses that turn. The second player draws a game card and proceeds in the same manner. Continue playing until one player reaches the "Winner" sign.

Memory Match

Players: 2 or more
Object: To collect the most pairs of cards
Materials: Pattern pages 282–292, scissors, construction paper, glue

Preparation: Reproduce two copies of the pattern pages. Mount the copies on construction paper and then cut apart the cards. Sort the cards into three sets. Reproduce four more copies of the Wild Card to complete the sets.

Directions: For this memory game, let the children decide which set of instruments they would like to use. To begin play, arrange the cards *face down* on a large flat surface in several rows. Have the first player turn two cards *face up*. If the cards match, the player identifies the instrument, keeps the cards, and then turns two more cards *face up*. If the cards do not match, the player turns the cards *face down* again. Be sure all players see the cards before they are returned to their original positions. The next player takes a turn to find matching pairs. If a Wild Card is turned over, the player collects both cards shown at that time. Continue playing until all possible matches have been made.

Music Maker Match

Players: 5 or less
Object: To cover all spaces on the bingo board
Materials: Pattern pages 282–284, 286, and 293–297, construction paper, white or colored copier paper, scissors, glue, game markers, clear adhesive tape

Preparation: Reproduce the pattern pages on white or colored copier paper. Mount the game boards and instrument picture cards on construction paper. Cut apart the cards. Discard the ukulele and the maracas picture cards. Decide how the students will play the game. If the student must identify the instrument by looking at the picture, provide game cards without labels. To do this, remove the name from the bottom of each card and tape it to the back. If the students are learning how to read the names of the instruments, provide the picture cards as shown on the pattern pages. Store the game pieces in a large envelope.

Directions: For this variation of bingo, give each student a Music Maker Match board. Place the game cards *face up* in a pile. To play a round, each student draws a game card and announces the name of the instrument.

All players check their game boards. If the name of the instrument is shown, the player marks the corresponding space. If the name is not shown, the player loses that turn. Continue playing until one player has marked all spaces on his or her game board.

Variation: If the players must identify each instrument, have the "Caller" hold the picture card so all players can see it. The player with the corresponding name on the game board must identify the instrument.

Call It! Instruments of the Orchestra

Players: 32 or less
Object: To answer all the clues as a team within a specified time
Materials: Pattern pages 298–305, construction paper/tagboard, glue, scissors, laminating material
Preparation: Photocopy the pattern pages and mount them on construction paper or tagboard. You may prefer to enlarge the game card pattern pages at 120% before photocopying the classroom set. When finished, laminate the cards for durability, if desired. Cut apart the game cards and store them in a large envelope.

Directions: For this fast action game (a round robin game) students must listen carefully to the clues and answer quickly. Each player will have an opportunity to answer a clue and read a new clue. The class must work as a team to finish the game within a predetermined length of time.

Distribute the cards to the students. If there are fewer than 32 students, encourage some students to select two cards. Decide what the time limit will be. To start the game, the player who holds the "violin" game card reads the first clue. The player who holds the corresponding instrument (cymbals) announces the answer and then reads out loud a different clue which is printed on the bottom of her or his card. Another player announces the correct answer and then quickly reads the next clue. Continue the game in this manner until all players have answered clues. If the game is completed within the time limit, the class wins the game. For an answer key, use the pattern pages to be sure the clues are answered correctly. To do this, just move from box to box.

Music Go Round

Players: 2 or 3
Object: To identify the instruments correctly to reach BRAVO!
Materials: Pattern pages 282–287 and 306, scissors, construction paper, glue, watercolor markers, game markers, envelope

Preparation: Duplicate pattern pages and mount them on construction paper. Color the game board as desired. Cut apart the game cards, removing the name from the bottom of each card. To make this game self-checking, provide the name of the instrument on the back of each card. Be sure to include a number from 1 to 4 on the back of the card. This will indicate how many spaces the player can move if the instrument is identified correctly. When finished, store the cards in an envelope.

Directions: Mix up the game cards and place them *face up* in a pile. Have each student select a game marker and place it on START. The first player draws a game card and identifies the instrument. If the answer is correct, the player moves his or her game marker the corresponding number of spaces (shown on the card) on the path. The second player takes a turn and plays in the same manner. When all game cards have been used, reshuffle and use again. Continue playing until one player reaches BRAVO!

Variation: Have the students identify the instruments by family.

Instrument Card Patterns

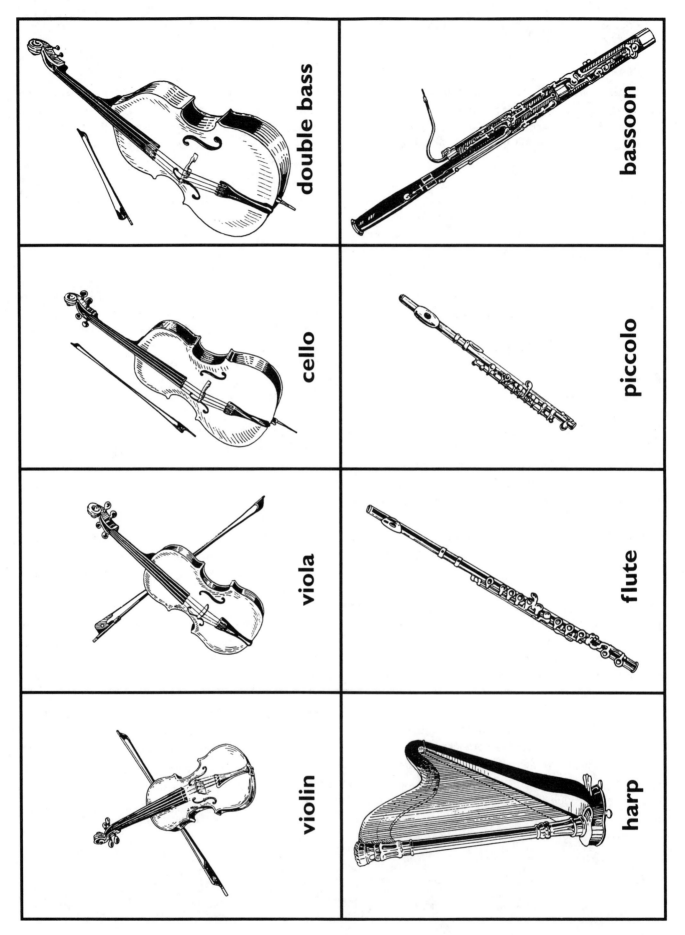

double bass

bassoon

cello

piccolo

viola

flute

violin

harp

Instrument Card Patterns

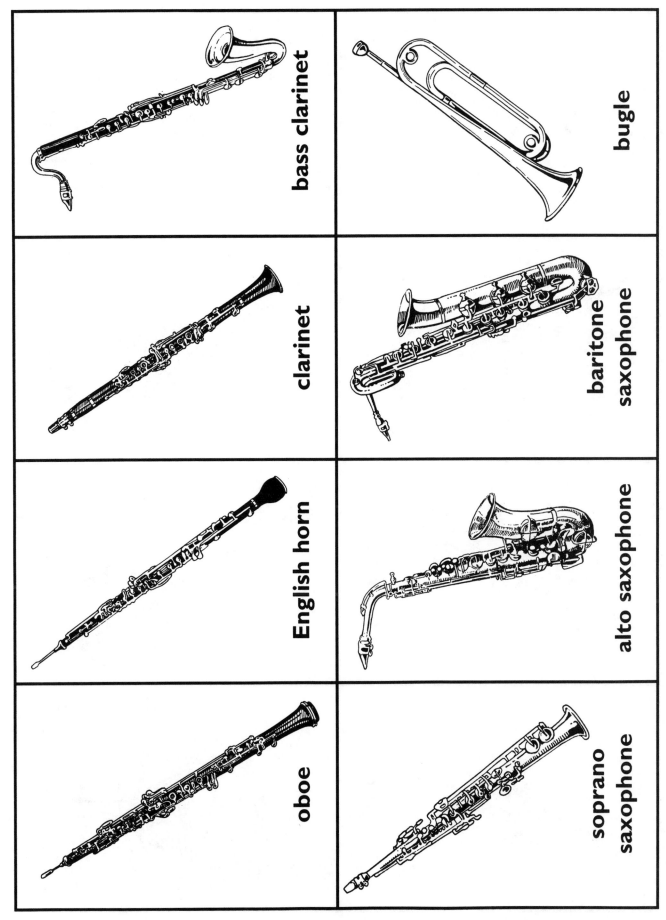

bass clarinet

bugle

clarinet

baritone saxophone

English horn

alto saxophone

oboe

soprano saxophone

Instrument Card Patterns

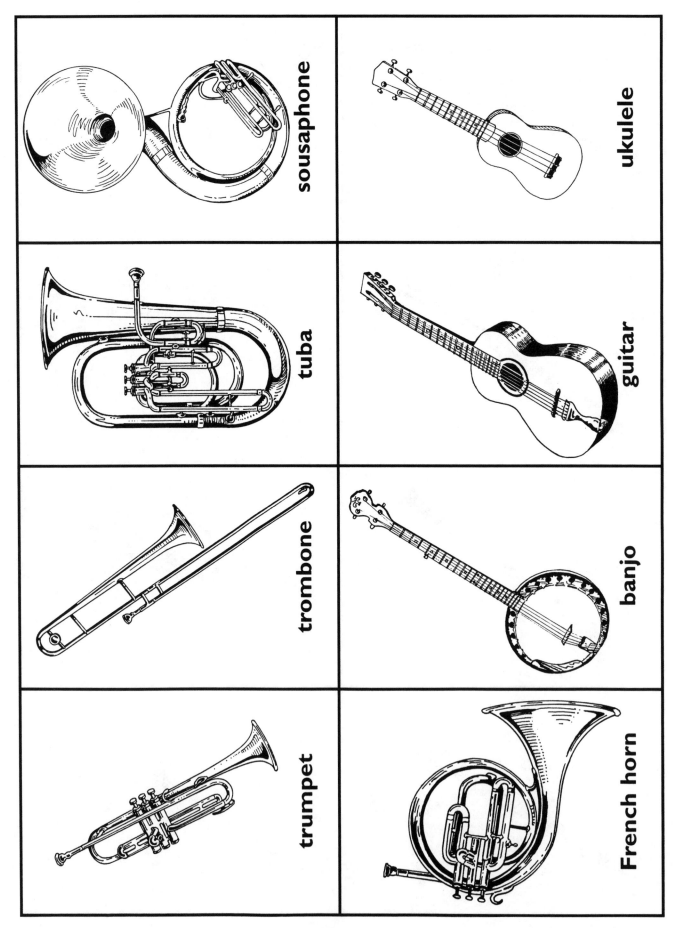

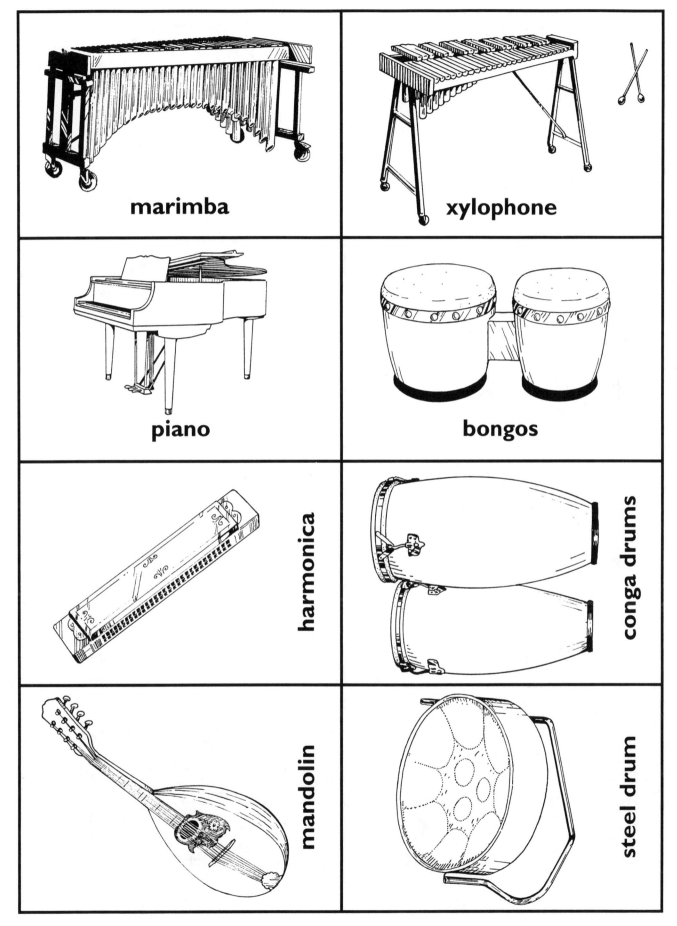

marimba

xylophone

piano

bongos

harmonica

conga drums

mandolin

steel drum

Instrument Card Patterns

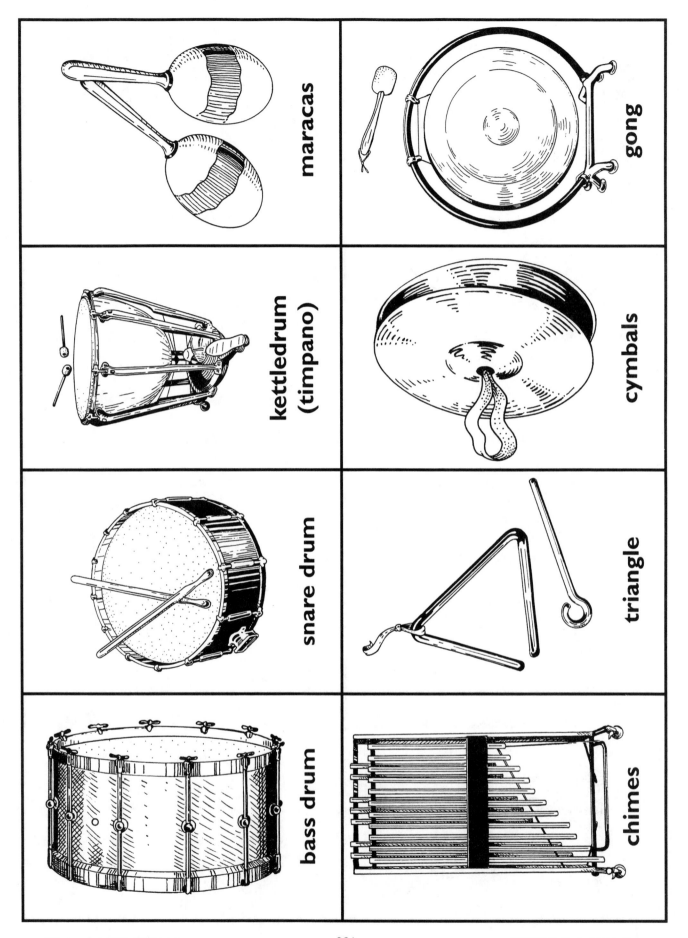

maracas

gong

kettledrum (timpano)

cymbals

snare drum

triangle

bass drum

chimes

IF20453 *Big Book of Music Games*

Instrument Card Patterns

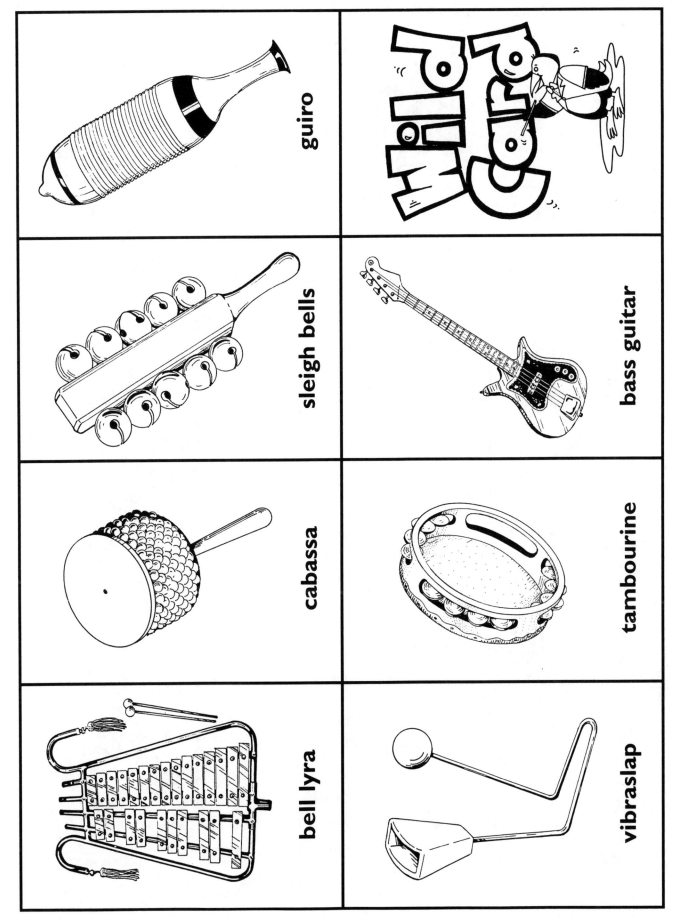

guiro

Wild Card

sleigh bells

bass guitar

cabassa

tambourine

bell lyra

vibraslap

Instrument Quest!

String Family	**String Family**	**String Family**
It is the smallest bowed instrument of the orchestra. (violin)	It looks like the violin but is larger in size. (viola)	It looks like the double bass but is smaller in size. (cello)
String Family	**String Family**	**Woodwind Family**
This large instrument stands six feet tall and is played with a bow. (double bass)	It has 47 strings which are plucked to make sound. (harp)	It is a long silver pipe with holes and finger keys. (flute)
Woodwind Family	**Woodwind Family**	**Woodwind Family**
About half the length of a flute, it makes very high shrill tones. (piccolo)	This nine-foot sound tube is doubled back and makes low nasal sounds. (bassoon)	It has a double-reed mouthpiece and a straight sound tube which makes a nasal sound. (oboe)
Woodwind Family	**Woodwind Family**	**Woodwind Family**
It is related to the oboe, however its sound tube ends with a bulge shape. (English horn)	About the same size as an oboe, it has a single-reed mouthpiece and a straight sound tube. (clarinet)	Its notes are an octave lower than the clarinet. This single-reed instrument is curved like a pipe. (bass clarinet)

Woodwind Family	**Woodwind Family**	**Woodwind Family**
This single-reed brass instrument has a straight sound tube. (soprano saxophone)	This single-reed brass instrument makes medium range tones. (alto saxophone)	Larger than the alto saxophone, this single-reed brass instrument makes low sounds. (baritone saxophone)
Brass Family	**Brass Family**	**Brass Family**
It is a small brass instrument which lacks valves. (bugle)	Brilliant high sounds are made by blowing through a six-foot tube of brass. It has three valves. (trumpet)	Its sound tube is made longer or shorter by moving its slide. This changes the pitch. (trombone)
Brass Family	**Brass Family**	**Brass Family**
It is the deepest-pitched brass instrument of the orchestra. (tuba)	This sound tube curls around the player's body and opens into a huge bell above the player's head. (sousaphone)	Related to old hunting horns, it has three valves and a flared bell. (French horn)
String Family "Plucked"	**String Family "Plucked"**	**String Family "Plucked"**
This small round body with a very long neck holds five strings. Its body is a small drum. (banjo)	Larger than the ukulele, it is played by plucking or strumming its six or twelve strings. (guitar)	It looks like a tiny guitar. (ukulele)

String Family "Plucked"	**Woodwind Family**	**Keyboard Family**
It has a pear-shaped body and narrow neck which holds eight or ten strings. (mandolin)	It is also called a mouth organ. (harmonica)	This large instrument has 88 keys which you strike with your fingers. (piano)
Percussion Family	**Percussion Family**	**Percussion Family**
Related to the xylophone, it has 49 to 52 sound bars which make a more mellow sound. (marimba)	Its wooden bars ring when tapped with hard mallets. It has short sound tubes which hang down from the frame. (xylophone)	These small drums are tapped with hands to produce sound. (bongos)
Percussion Family	**Percussion Family**	**Percussion Family**
Its metal drumhead makes bright sounds when tapped with drumsticks. (steel drum)	These tall drums are larger than bongos. Players use their hands to make short sounds. (conga drums)	This large drum stands upright on its side. A soft mallet is used to make sound. (bass drum)
Percussion Family	**Percussion Family**	**Percussion Family**
This side drum has snares which vibrate when the drumhead is tapped with drumsticks. (snare drum)	It is the only pitched drum in the orchestra. (kettledrum)	These two rattles are filled with grains. (maracas)

Percussion Family It is also called the glockenspiel. It sounds like bells. (bell lyra)	**Percussion Family** A long string of silver steel beads is wrapped around the body of the instrument. (cabassa)	**Percussion Family** It has small bells that are attached to a wooden stick. (sleigh bells)
Percussion Family This gourd-shaped hollow instrument makes sound when rubbed with a stick. (guiro)	**Percussion Family** A wooden ball hits a cowbell shape to make a special sound. (vibraslap)	**Percussion Family** This handheld drum has metal discs which rattle when shaken. (tambourine)
Electronic Family It has four strings which are plucked to make deep sounds. (bass guitar)	**Percussion Family** Very long metal tubes hang from a frame and sound like bells when tapped with a mallet. (chimes)	**Percussion Family** A single metal bar is bent to make this instrument. (triangle)
Percussion Family When these two brass plates are clashed together, a loud ringing sound is made. (cymbals)	**Percussion Family** This huge metal plate shape hangs from a frame and is tapped with a mallet. (gong)	**Take a rest!**

Music Maker Match

clarinet	cymbals	violin	oboe
chimes	bass drum	soprano saxophone	flute
cello	banjo	guitar	bugle

IF20453 *Big Book of Music Games*

Music Maker Match

chimes	gong	bass clarinet	snare drum
oboe	viola	banjo	trumpet
piccolo	baritone saxophone	tuba	double bass

3

Music Maker Match

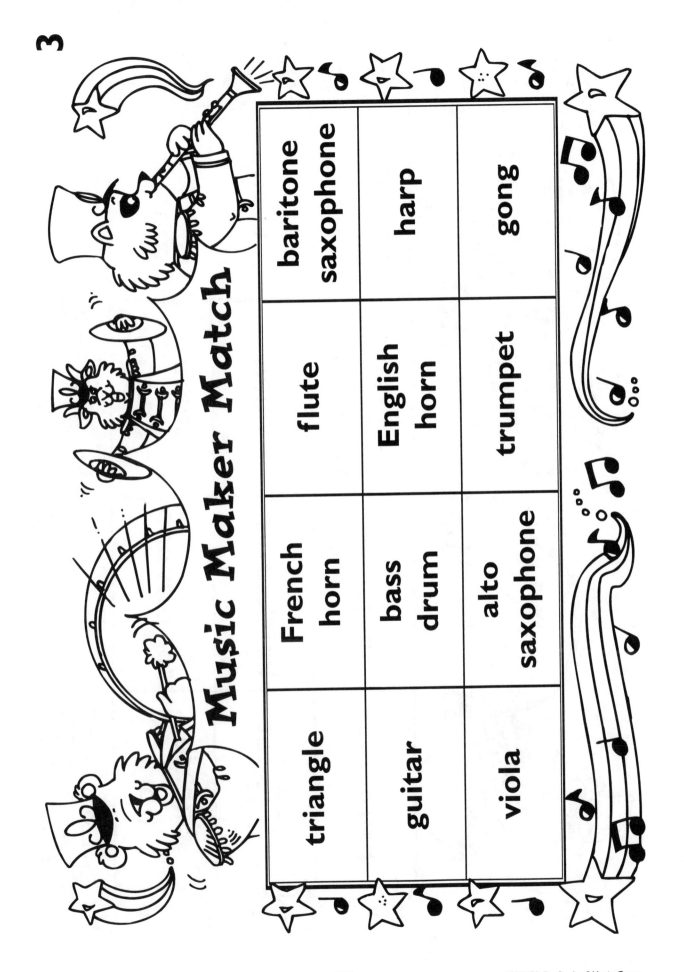

baritone saxophone	flute	French horn	triangle
harp	English horn	bass drum	guitar
gong	trumpet	alto saxophone	viola

4

Music Maker Match

trombone	bassoon	soprano saxophone	double bass
bass clarinet	kettledrum	violin	tuba
English horn	sousaphone	snare drum	triangle

Music Maker Match

clarinet	cello	kettledrum
harp	trombone	bugle
cymbals	French horn	bassoon
alto saxophone		
sousaphone		
piccolo		

IF20453 Big Book of Music Games

Answer: violin

Clue:
They look like round brass plates.

Answer: cymbals

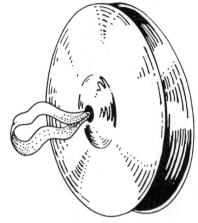

Clue:
This single-reed woodwind is about the same size as an oboe.

Answer: clarinet

Clue:
This giant string instrument makes low bullfrog tones.

Answer: double bass

Clue:
This brass instrument has a slide instead of valves.

Answer: trombone

Clue:
This double-reed instrument has an onion-shaped bell.

Answer: English horn

Clue:
Inside these gourd-shaped instruments are grains which rattle when shaken.

Answer: maracas

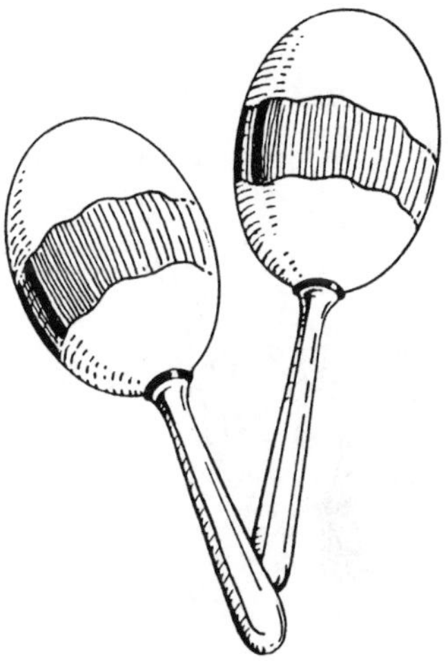

Clue:
It looks like an old hunting horn, however, it has three valves.

Answer: French horn

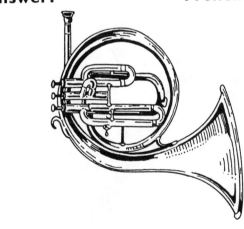

Clue:
When its 47 strings are plucked, beautiful gentle sounds can be heard.

Answer: harp

Clue:

This very large double-reed instrument looks like a narrow pole.

Answer: bassoon

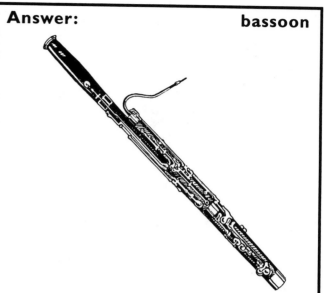

Clue:

Longer than a piccolo, it looks like a silver pipe.

Answer: flute

Clue:

This giant percussion instrument is the only pitched drum.

Answer: kettledrum (timpano)

Clue:

This bowed instrument is held upright between the knees when played.

Answer: cello

Clue:
Bright high-pitched sounds can be made with this brass instrument.

Answer: trumpet

Clue:
Related to the clarinet, this instrument makes deeper tones.

Answer: bass clarinet

Clue:
Shorter than the English horn, this woodwind is known for its clear nasal tones.

Answer: oboe

Clue:
Hard mallets are used to strike the wooden bars that rest on its frame.

Answer: xylophone

Clue:

It is the largest and lowest-pitched brass instrument in the orchestra.

Answer: tuba

Clue:

Shrill sounds are made by this very short silver pipe.

Answer: piccolo

Clue:

Played with a bow, this instrument is a little larger than the violin.

Answer: viola

Clue:

It is a small flat drum which is tapped or shaken to make sound.

Answer: tambourine

Clue:
While hanging from a string, this metal bar is tapped with a metal striker.

Answer: triangle

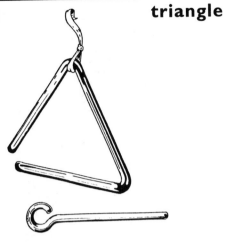

Clue:
Its long metal tubes make bell sounds when tapped with a mallet.

Answer: chimes

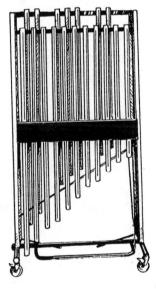

Clue:
It has snares which vibrate when the drumhead is tapped.

Answer: snare drum

Clue:
This single-reed instrument is made of brass.

Answer: saxophone

Clue:

A loud rumble is heard when this huge metal plate is tapped repeatedly.

Answer: gong

Clue:

Standing upright on its side, it makes deep "booms" when tapped by a mallet.

Answer: bass drum

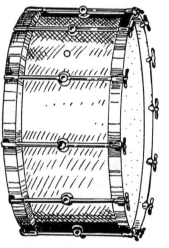

Clue:

It has small bells attached to a piece of wood.

Answer: sleigh bells

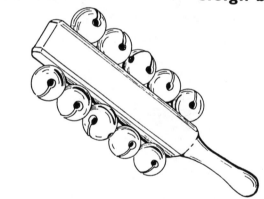

Clue:

This small instrument has a wooden ball that hits a small cowbell shape.

Answer: vibraslap

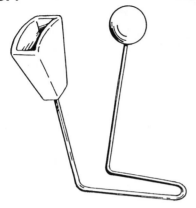

Clue:
This very large instrument has 88 strings and a keyboard.

Answer: piano

Clue:
A handheld instrument, strands of silver beads circle around its body.

Answer: cabassa

Clue:
This small percussion instrument makes a scraping sound.

Answer: guiro

Clue:
Smaller than the viola, it is the highest-pitched string instrument.

Let's Meet
Famous Composers

Let's Meet Famous Composers

Classy Composers

Players: 2 or 3
Object: The first player to reach AWESOME is the winner.
Materials: Pattern pages 309–311, 314–315, and 318–319, glue, colored file folder, construction paper, scissors, game markers, watercolor markers

Preparation: Photocopy the pattern pages. To prepare the game cards, mount pages 309–311 on construction paper, then cut apart the game cards. To make the game cards self-checking, mount the clue card for a composer on the back of the corresponding picture card. Be sure to remove the answer on the clue card before adhering it. Continue in the same manner until all clue cards have been glued to picture cards. Be sure to include a number from 1 to 4 on the picture side of the card. This will indicate how many spaces the player can move if the composer is identified correctly. For the game board, mount the pages 318-319 on the file folder. Be sure to align the path to complete the scene.

Directions: Have two students place the game board and clue cards within reach. Arrange the clue cards in a pile so the pictures are *face down*. Decide which player will start the round. The first player draws a clue card and identifies the composer. If the answer is correct, the player moves his or her game marker the corresponding number of spaces. If the answer is incorrect, the player loses that turn. The second player draws a game card and proceeds in the same manner. Continue playing until one player reaches AWESOME.

Variations: You may wish to write clue cards that reflect the information covered in class. For more information and activities about these composers, refer to *Let's Meet Famous Composers* (Instructional Fair•TS Denison). Other composer cards can be prepared and used. See pattern pages 312-313 and 316-317.

Composer Memory Match

Players: 2 or more
Object: To collect the most pairs of cards
Materials: Pattern pages 282–292, scissors, construction paper, glue

Preparation: Reproduce two copies of the pattern pages. Mount the copies on construction paper and then cut apart the cards. Sort the cards into three sets. Be sure to include a pair of Wild Cards in each set.

Directions: Play the game in the same manner as "Instrument Memory Match."

Music Quest!

Players: 2 or 3
Object: To identify the composer correctly to reach BRAVO!
Materials: Pattern pages 312–313, 316–317, and 320, glue, scissors, construction paper, game markers

Preparation: Duplicate pattern pages and mount pages 312-313 and 320 on construction paper. Cut apart the game cards. To make the game cards self-checking, mount the clue card for a composer on the back of the corresponding picture card. Be sure to remove the answer on the clue card before adhering it. Continue in the same manner until all clue cards are prepared.

Directions: Play the game in the same manner as "Classy Composers."

Variation: Other composer cards can be prepared and used. You may wish to write clue cards that reflect the information covered in class. For more information and activities about these composers, refer to *Classical Music Stories* (Instructional Fair•TS Denison).

Johann Sebastian Bach

Ludwig van Beethoven

Johannes Brahms

Frederic Chopin

George Gershwin

George Frederick Handel

Franz Joseph Haydn

Franz Liszt

Fanny Mendelssohn

Felix Mendelssohn

Wolfgang Amadeus Mozart

Franz Peter Schubert

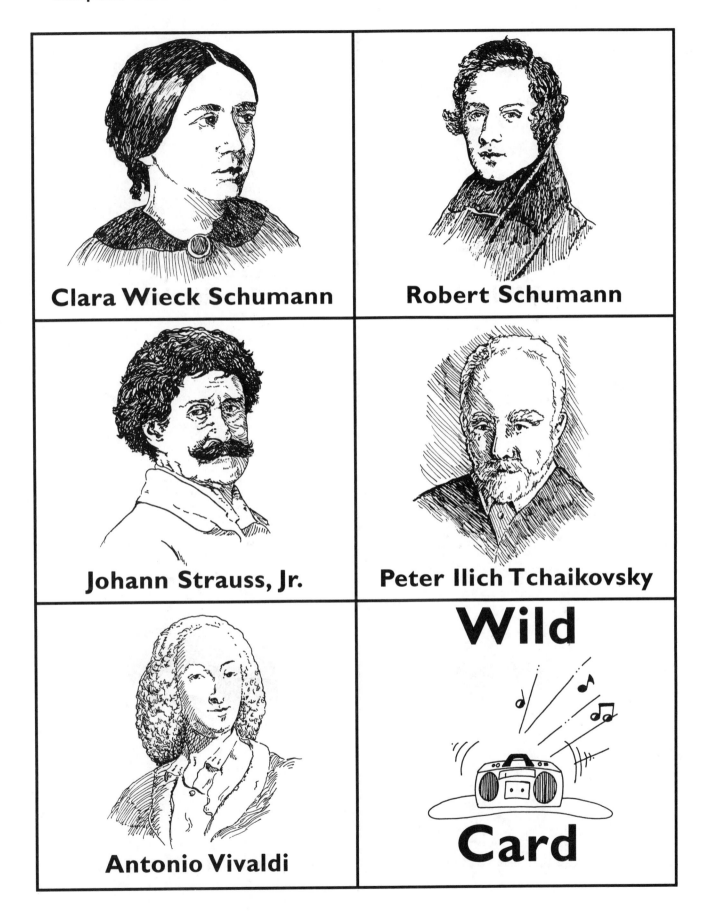

Clara Wieck Schumann

Robert Schumann

Johann Strauss, Jr.

Peter Ilich Tchaikovsky

Antonio Vivaldi

Wild

Card

B. B. King

Benjamin Britten

Aaron Copland

Paul Dukas

Edvard Grieg

Gustav Holst

Edward "Duke" Ellington

Sergei Prokofiev

Camille Saint-Saëns

Leonard Bernstein

• Born the same year as G. F. Handel (1685) • Excellent violinist, harpsichord player, organist, as well as composer (Bach)	• Also composed when deaf • First composer to earn a living from his music • Wrote *Pastoral (Sixth) Symphony* (Beethoven)	• Kept a life-long friendship with Robert and Clara Schumann • Known for "Brahms' Lullaby" (Brahms)
• Called "The Poet of the Piano" • Made the piano a solo instrument • Grew up in the country of Poland (Chopin)	• Wrote the first American opera, "Porgy and Bess" • American composer who used jazz and classical music together (Gershwin)	• Born the same year as J. S. Bach (1685) • Composed the *Messiah* which people still perform (Handel)
• Called "Father of the Orchestra" • Close friend and teacher of W. A. Mozart • Wrote *Surprise Symphony* (Haydn)	• First pianist to turn the piano sideways so the audience could watch the hands strike the keys • Famous in Europe during 1800s (Liszt)	• Wrote 6 songs that were published by her younger brother in his name (Fanny Mendelssohn)

Classy Composer Clue Cards

• Wrote the *Midsummer Night's Dream* overture at age 17 • Accomplished pianist, composer, and conductor (Felix Mendelssohn)	• Was a child composer and performer • Wrote the opera *The Magic Flute* • Wrote first song at age 5 (Mozart)	• Wrote over 600 *lieder* (German art songs) • Elementary teacher for 3 years • Composed "Ave Maria" (Schubert)
• Talented pianist • Married Robert Schumann • First pianist to play entire concerts by memory (Clara Schumann)	• Wrote some of his best piano music for children who are learning to play the piano • Married his piano teacher's daughter (Robert Schumann)	• Became known as the "Waltz King" • Wrote over 400 waltzes, such as "On the Beautiful Blue Danube" (Strauss, Jr.)
• Russian composer who composed the ballets *The Nutcracker* and *Sleeping Beauty* • Also known for symphonies (Tchaikovsky)	• Italian composer and ordained priest whose nickname was "Red Priest" • Composed *The Four Seasons* (Vivaldi)	**Take a rest!**

Music Quest! Clue Cards

Composed the tune "In a Sentimental Mood" (Ellington)	Performed with electric guitar and popularized music known as the "blues" (King)	Composed *The Young Person's Guide to the Orchestra* (Britten)
Composed *Appalachian Spring* (Copeland)	Composed *The Sorcerer's Apprentice* (Dukas)	Composed *Peer Gynt Suites* (Grieg)
Composed *The Planets* (Op. 32) (Holst)	Composed *Peter and the Wolf* (Prokofiev)	Composed *The Carnival of the Animals* (Saint-Saëns)
Wrote the music for the Broadway musical "West Side Story" (Bernstein)	**Take a rest!**	**Move ahead 2 spaces!**

Created his own style of jazz Wrote over 1,000 tunes, such as "Satin Doll" and "Cottontail" (Ellington)	Shortened his name to B. B. which stood for "Blues Boy" (King)	Wrote a composition to introduce children to the symphony and the four families of instruments (Britten)
Used folk music in his compositions, such as the tune "The Gift to Be Simple" in *Appalachian Spring* (Copeland)	A French composer who used the orchestra to describe a story about a Sorcerer's apprentice (Dukas)	Wrote the background music for the play "Peer Gynt" Paid about $200 for the music (Grieg)
His most important orchestral piece described the planets through music (Holst)	Wrote music about a boy named Peter and a wolf to introduce the instruments of the orchestra (Prokofiev)	His composition used 2 pianos and orchestra to describe the lion, rooster, mules, elephant, and so on (Saint-Saëns)
Talented conductor and American composer who wrote music for Broadway musicals (Bernstein)	**Draw again.**	**Move ahead 2 spaces!**

Start

"CLASSY"

Awesome

COMPOSERS

Music Quest!

Bravo!

Start

IF20453 Big Book of Music Games